Just Like the Blitz

Just Like the Blitz

A Reporter's Notebook

Derek Lambert

HAMISH HAMILTON
LONDON

First published in Great Britain 1987 by
Hamish Hamilton Ltd
27 Wrights Lane London W8 5TZ
Copyright © 1987 by Derek Lambert
British Library Cataloguing in Publication Data

Lambert, Derek
Just like the Blitz.
1. Authors, English—20th century—Biography
2. Journalists—Great Britain—Biography
i. Title
070'.92'4   PR6062.A47Z/

ISBN 0–241–12343–7

Typeset by Pentacor Ltd, High Wycombe
Printed in Great Britain by
Redwood Burn Ltd, Trowbridge Wiltshire

PREFACE

Dear Diary. . . . Why do we do it? Chronicle daily, or even periodically, the sometimes jaunty, occasionally anguished and often mundane incidents in our lives. Hard-nosed egotism perhaps; a purging of our inadequacies; anticipation of a day when from our wheelchairs we will be able to remuster lost youth. . . .

Ever since Pepys psychologists have proffered obvious explanations, honest dishes garnished with the requisite obscurity. What would they make of the diarist who, 22 years after his private indulgence, seeks to publish his chronicles?

A touch of exhibitionism certainly. A possibility that even more than two decades ago I may have slyly envisaged a time when a bold publisher would agree to print my reflections. Hopefully, although I may be deluding myself, there are two more creditable notions.

The diaries, mostly typed on newsprint cut-offs, came to light in the conventional manner − discovered in an attic clear-out, although without the extraordinary degree of astonishment that seems to visit novelists when they stumble across a forgotten manuscript. And it occurred to me that they might contain two bonuses, one historical, the other sociological.

Sociological. Representatives of the media are today under attack just as much as they were in my day. Mostly, now as then, by those whose deceits have been exposed or by those who seek to burnish lacklustre personalities with moral outrage.

My four-year record of endeavour does, I feel, help to acquaint the reader with the realities of a profession in which cynicism is more often than not a refuge from compassion, in which — with extravagant exceptions — accuracy is deified, in which the pursuit of justice is the ultimate trail. And may the wrath of the great Editor in the Sky descend upon all those seekers of public recognition who, having achieved it, turn upon the scribes who helped to elevate them.

The diaries may also enlighten the public about the fluctuations and hazards of a reporter's life and, perhaps, elicit a measure of understanding. Not that there is anything masochistic about the calling — every day is a novel and it is a sad day for publicans when the journalists pack up their anecdotes and move elsewhere on the current of economics — but, domestically, it can be destructive: being-kept-late-at-the-office can be prolonged for as long as three months.

Historically. The period that I partially recorded tends to be dismissed as the Swinging Sixties. In fact it was a significant decade because it contained the seeds of regression which, although disguised by electronic sleight of hand, is the hallmark of the eighties. The principal culprits were the middle-aged and elderly arbiters of morals who, fearfully anticipating the ridicule of the young, encouraged the first sniggers of permissiveness and closed their ears to the warning shots of violence on television.

Regression? Who can doubt it? Exploration of space has been largely abortive and we have reverted to parochial endeavour on our tiny globe in which dreary and fallible computers rule. But regression is not necessarily deterioration. AIDS, the greatest reformer of morals this century, has taught us that promiscuity can kill; drugs, tobacco and alcohol all stand accused of wholesale murder. Could it be that, having reached a peak of evolution, we are now descending to more comfortable levels of moderation?

How many young people in the sixties would have believed that, 20 years on, their lookalikes might dine with a sexual partner they had chosen for life and drink mineral water in candlelight unadorned by a single skein of cigarette smoke? Certainly not me.

These entries, then, provide a glimpse of an era with its half-forgotten wars, scandals, statesmen and strolling players, in which the watershed of the eighties had its beginnings. Whether such laudable motives were ever envisaged by the diarist is dubious; probably his concern was self-satisfaction, accompanied by the apologia that one day his indulgence might provide enjoyment for others.

1962

October 18.
The fog lifts, leaving London quick with bronzed light and expectation. For me a jigsaw day. I am despatched first to a small factory in Acton where 40 women make hair shampoos containing beer. The sunshine invests the suburbs with fragile graces.

The women are a formidable team surrounded by pans of coloured soap and pints of best bitter. But they have been upset by a van driver who, doubting their sporting acumen, withdrew from their football pools syndicate. In retaliation they sent him to Coventry and today, beaten and bowed, he pinned an apology on the notice-board.

The boss has also pinned up a letter pleading with the shampoo ladies to settle their differences with the presumptuous driver in view of the Christmas rush. They agree with majestic grace to forgive him. Over lunch — fish and chips washed down with half pints of beer which is dispensed free — one woman with dimpled elbows confides: 'Bloody cheek. Football? He doesn't know Arsenal from arseholes.'

Later I am sent to St. Thomas's Hospital where a porter has been sacked for taking photographs of a nude girl lab assistant. As he says: 'Some people collect stamps, I photograph naked girls. More interesting than penny blacks any day.' The hospital secretary warns me not to take his lyrical view of nudity too seriously. I accompany the porter

1

to his basement flat – divan, sink, two TV sets and a Spanish girl-friend. He shows me the pictures of the lab assistant proudly displaying her charms. He tells me girls are quite willing to strip for him in his dungeon. And to think I've been collecting stamps all these years.

October 21.
I dash into a Fleet Street pub for a Sunday-lunch pint after spending the morning looking for actress Dawn Addams to be told: 'Catch the 5.40 plane to Calcutta.' The plan is for me to fly on to Tezpur in Assam where the Indian Army, fighting the Chinese invaders swarming over the Himalayas, has its HQ. There aren't many jobs in which you can be wallowing in beer shampoo one day and off to confront Chairman Mao's warriors the next.

Athens breezy, Cairo steamy. Beside me sits a pretty girl with auburn hair who is flying home to Australia. She didn't like England, Englishmen or Englishwomen. The men, she says, were pale and crude in their sexual advances and the women were twee. At Karachi we are joined by an American who keeps asking his wife why she hasn't taken her travel pills. 'But Jesus God, Martha, you know how you get.' She does and reaches for a paper-bag. At Calcutta I bid farewell to the Australian girl. Pale I may be, crude never!

October 22.
I take a cab from Dum Dum airport into Calcutta. It's only 2 pm but there are beds on the roadside containing inert bodies; others sleep on the pavement as if they've suddenly folded up there. Old men lugubriously dare traffic to hit them; semi-naked boys poke their navels ruminatively; rickshaws dodge hump-backed cattle; families spill from currugated-iron huts and leaning tenements; stagnant ponds bloom with mauve lilies. Finally we reach the Great Eastern Hotel, a cool and spacious pile inprisoning echoes of the Raj. The beer in the bar tastes of soap. Is there no escape from Acton?

2

October 23.

A perilous ride through the waking suburbs, to the airport.
'Definitely not − I am telling you absolutely definitely not,'
says Peter Sellers Indian in reply to my request for a seat on
the Tezpur-bound plane. 'Absolutely definitely, yes,' says
another irritably. 'I shall be asking you to wait and see,' says
the first with dignity. I meet the Maharajah of Cooch Behar,
lithe playboy in the best Aly Khan tradition, who is waiting
for another plane. Judging by his limp he has been playing
too much lately. With him is his English wife, blonde and
cool, in a pink sari. We all get seats on our planes.

My Dakota puts down sharply at Tezpur, my ears pop
painfully as we lose altitude. A young teaplanter, thin with
bright blue eyes in a tanned face, drives me to a desserted
station club − Victorian with becalmed brown furniture.
With him is a curly-haired girl, sensible and British, who has
joined him for a two-month stay. She lives at Beckenham
and carries tennis rackets with her.

I tour the town in the oldest taxi in the world. The driver
appears to be running through a hole in the floor. A bald
district commissioner greets me: 'Good morning, how are
you? Did you go to Oxford or Cambridge University?' and
regards me suspiciously when I say neither; but he is better
company than the educated young Indian I dined with in
Calcutta who kept announcing he could think of nine four-
letter swear words and did I want to hear them. I didn't but I
was disgruntled because I couldn't think of anything like
nine.

I meet a chunky American Baptist minister and his wife at
their hospital outside Tezpur. He is very American, very
Baptist, very good. He is worried about his wife and children
as the Chinese advance through thr North East Frontier
mountains quicker than the pundits anticipated.

I manage to cable a story from a primitive telegraph office
but am doubtful if it will reach Calcutta let alone London. I
meet Ed Behr from *Time* and Drew Pearson from NBC. We
buy tins of sausages and beans from the club shop and ask a
servant to heat them up. Revolting. There is no room in the

3

club and I sleep in a building called an inspection bungalow, sharing a room with mosquitoes and an Indian who thinks my 10.30pm arrival is an assassination attempt. I wash in a bucket and let down the mosquito net, adroitly trapping squadrons of mosquitoes in bed with me.

October 24.

I drive with Pearson, short, American and friendly, in a taxi to the foothills through apple-green paddy fields and jungle. The only troops we meet are marching away from the fighting. We pass several check points with surprising ease until authority clamps down at a camp called Foothills. While one police officer tells Drew that he is not allowed to make any statement to the Press another one gives me the Chinese positions. They are 17 miles from Tawang, a monastery town inhabited by lamas and peaceful tribesmen who make carpets and love horses (guide book). Anyway, their days of peace are numbered. We meet a commissioner who regrets we cannot go farther. 'I am very sorry and I would like to take you for a picnic but things are not so damn good.'

Back to the club after angry police at Foothills discover that our driver hasn't got a license. We read the local daily paper and learn that America has imposed a blockade on Russian arms entering Cuba. So my story leaves the front page.

Drew and I decide that evening to escape sausages and beans and take a bicycle rickshaw to a restaurant next to a flea-pit cinema. We swoop past tiny shops and candle-lit stalls; fireflies sparkle in the dark, the sky is thick with stars. In the open-air restaurant we are served a meal consisting of skinny chicken dripping with rancid curry paste and sweet bread washed down with orange juice that tastes of cart grease. My appetite isn't improved by an Indian who squashes a beetle as big as a vole with his bare foot. We take in an Indian film all about fixed marriage compications. The hero gets blown up twice, looses and regains his memory and finds time to sing several unmelodious love songs. We leave scratching.

4

Back at the club a drunken Indian journalist is in the middle of a tirade. He keeps insisting: 'It is all balls. I am sorry but I am going to have to say it again − it is all balls.' He is now on his upteenth whisky; a desperate figure with a pencil moustache and wild, thinning hair. The object of his fury is a taxi driver who took him round the paddy fields and made an exorbitant charge. Suddenly he begins to apologise abjectly and, clutching a glass of diluted whisky, accompanies me to the cable office. He insists on reading my cable, pronounces it 'All balls' and vanishes into the night.

October 25.
Tezpur is a pretty town by day. Tall rustling trees, hollows of grassland, gentle goats wandering the baked streets beneath a luminous sky awash with fragments of cloud. I interview an Indian officer who gives me a good story about the fall of Tawang. I file a story well ahead of the official release but I'm still not sure of cable delays.

Later the desperate Indian challenges me to a game of billiards in the club. After every other shot he apologises for unapparent misdemeanours and accepts my congratulations for good shots with rapturous thank yous. Diluted whisky slops onto the floor and his shots become wilder and more successful as he drinks. He wins and, as the balls click for the last time, he remarks: 'It is all a lot of balls really.' And I suppose this time he is right.

October 26.
Lunch with the American Baptist minister, his wife, their two children and two American correspondents. It's the first decent meal I've eaten in India.

They live in an airy house in the hospital grounds surrounded by lots of grass and tall trees. They radiate goodness but do not preach.

The Press corps has been joined by a sad, dedicated American agency man. He frowns at my slightest sally and I feel like a blue-nosed comic at Sadlers Wells. He is large and slow and undoubtedly 100 per cent accurate. I only wish he

5

would make a joke so I could make a point of not laughing at it. I am relieved at arrival of an ITN cameraman I knew in the Congo. We drink beer together and meet 78-year-old Anglican padre Wyld who is unimpressed by the Chinese advance: he is concerned only with launching an indoor tennis game that he proposes to call Tez Tennis. The wild Indian journalist says the war is all over. Fighting is 'all a lot of balls'.

October 27.
Diwali, festival of lights. Outside each hut, each shop, hang rows of earthenware lamps filled with mustard-seed oil. The lamps flicker, fireflies sparkle, stars glimmer and fire crackers explode, tiny echoes of the gunfire in the mountains.

October 28.
We drive with two ITN journalists through the jungle to the foothills looking optimistically for refugees. The jungle is a wall of creeper-hung undergrowth starred with mauve and white blossoms; hand-sized butterflies flap past and insects drone busily. Hill people, stringy and Mongolian-featured, stare at us and wave sheepishly; we wave back sheepishly. We find no refugees and return to soapy beer, beans and sausages.

Lock myself out of the bedroom. Drew, who is small, climbs in through a window. I try but get one buttock and half my private parts stuck. This amuses an Indian boy who refuses to go away. Drew breaks the lock and after a painful withdrawal in which my parts become an endangered species I collapse in bed where the mosquitoes welcome me back.

October 29.
News non-existent. Over the radio we hear the astonishing news that Krushchev has agreed to the dismantling of Cuban missile bases.

We adjourn to Padre Wyld's. He plays records on an ancient gramophone with a horn that could accommodate three Master's Voice terriers. 'Come into the Garden

Maude,' a selection from *Lilac Time* and 'My Dear Old Dutch'. These records wheeze and groan until the padre revitalises them with frantic revolutions of the handle. Webster Booth and Ann Ziegler warble in cacophonous embrace, a wavering violin is joined outside by the barking of a jackal. The padre, a fragment of humanity, sits on the other side of the Tez Tennis court conducting yesterday's orchestras and singers, face rhapsodic, gold teeth gleaming.

Thus it has been for 27 years, in this Victorian, Edwardian, bungalow. And all for what? A few converts, a duty done, a calling fulfilled? 'We've been togather now for forty years . . . ' Sad and sweet he beats time, remembering heaven knows what. Afterwards he gives me prospectus for Tez Tennis and, thank the Lord, invites me to dinner next day.

October 30.
A drizzling, dripping Sunday. The sky is November-grey, the rain soft and incessant. It is a day to eat muffins and read cosy autobiographies in front of the fire — only there are no muffins, no autobiographies, no fires. In the evening we manage to see Lieut.-General Kaul, a firecracker of a man, with a bronchial cough who repeatedly asserts: 'We are going to give them bloody hell.' He is 50, smallish, delicately built and yet wiry. He has circumvented bureaucrats to see us; he tells us not to divulge our meeting and appears to be enjoying the secrecy. He was an outspoken anti-Communist put out to pasture because of his views: now his views have reluctantly been accepted and he has been recalled.

Later some of us pick our way across grass in the dark to the Baptists in hope of being offered some food. We get a slice of pudding and two cups of coffee. We have an interesting discussion with an American doctor who says we should watch out for snakes at night; if one does bite you and you are still living after thirty minutes then you are not going to die. The Baptists are eager for news and unclerical companionship.

7

October 31.

All-out war on mosquitoes. I spray the room with Flit, light joss sticks, none of which is appreciated by unbitten Drew. Why do they bite me and not him? Does he smell or do I?

During the evening Drew and I adjourn to the home of Padre Wyld. He leads us straight to his indoor tennis court. Tez Tennis is played with a net, ping-pong ball and large wooden bats like frying pans. We slip around with agility but the padre is more agile than us. I devise a method of walloping the ball very hard onto the wall so that it rebounds onto the court; this seems to discourage the padre who has to buy the balls in Calcutta and fears I may crack them.

November 1.

Krishna Menon, sacked the previous day as Defence Minister, arrives in Tezpur to give a fund-raising pep talk to a crowd of pigtailed schoolgirls and jostling boys. Menon broods during supporting speeches, leonine, beaky-nosed. He has a fine head with crinkly grey hair and deep-set eyes. An idealist's head − now a mask because the ideals are lost.

Sixty-five miles away the Chinese who have betrayed him are killing his countrymen. The schoolgirls are pretty, shy, with beads in their noses and ribbons in their polished hair. Big brown eyes gaze at me, elbows nudge, voices pipe and twitter prettily. Later I meet Menon. He is friendly, cagey, delighted to talk about irrelevant subjects such as incidence of peptic ulcers in the Army. Show me the politician who isn't friendly and cagey; except of course those who are unfriendly and cagey. No, he wasn't surprised by his demotion. Nor was anyone else.

November 3.

Other correspondents are now arriving. Anthony Mann, *Daily Telegraph*, flew in from Rome via Delhi; Ed Behr from *Time* returned; my smooth old friend from Nairobi days, Arthur Cook, of the *Daily Mail*, is alleged to be on his way; also John Tidmarsh, BBC, whom I last saw in Oran. I lunch with the padre on Irish stew made with goat meat.

In the evening AP and ITN reporters and myself drive out to a planters' club 15 miles from Tezpur. A young planter, porky and pompous, says: 'Look here, I've got a bone to pick with you chaps. Distorting the truth, making chaps' families worried back in Blighty.' As usual we ran into quite a lot of this — in fact they might have been banana growers in the Cameroons. At first I try reason — most of them haven't read the stories anyway — then sarcasm and finally rudeness. Instead of receiving a bunch of tannic knuckles on my nose I get: 'Of course I didn't necessarily mean *your* articles, old chap — have a drink.'

Their club is spacious, fanned by a breeze blowing across the paddy fields; it contains two billiard tables, old prints on the walls, photographs of a bewildered leopard ambling through undergrowth, and a smelly latrine. The prints and the smells were there with the Raj; so were the planters, or their fathers or grandfathers. One tea planter confesses to me: 'I'm afraid this is the only club in the valley where there are no affairs going on.'

November 4.
An improvised game of cricket — or it may have been baseball. We play with the thick end of a sawn-off billiards cue and an India-rubber ball. ITN and myself play some cool off-drives; the Americans clout the ball over the clubhouse. I file a story about lost soldiers emerging from the mountains — the troops missing after the initial retreat.

November 6.
Tiresome arrangements and cables about accreditation for a trip up to the front. By the time we depart the war will be over. That's probably the idea. John Tidmarsh of the BBC phones me from Guahati. He is on his way. I ask him to bring a cricket bat and some edible delicacies. In return I arrange accommodation for him with the padre. A worried colonel announces that if/when the trip comes off there will be no cameras. He also says that cables will have to go to Delhi for censorship.

9

A reminiscent evening with the padre — dinner is now a regular occurrence — with a piano recital of World War I songs and records of Melba, the Kentucky Minstrels and Churchill. The Churchill record takes me back to the balding lawn of my childhood home in Banstead, being summoned from a bonfire to listen to those muscular tones. Planes droning overhead, anti-splinter goo on the windows, vegetables in the flowerbed. I read a 1942 *Punch*.

November 9.
Tidmarsh arrives with bat and delicacies. I have a breezy drink with him, play a breezy game of billiards and a breezy game of cricket. We now hear that we are leaving for the front a 4am, Sunday, staying three days. The prospect of filing from the rickety cable office with dozens of competing journalists is depressing.

I dine with the padre and afterwards walk in the moonlight along the shores of the Brahmaputra to a currugated tin temple where a week-long feast is in progress. Lots of wailing and beating of drums, dancing not unlike the twist, a hermit almost naked and covered in ash. Carved in the rock is a scarlet-painted goddess. The atmosphere is convivial: cows doze among the sparks fanned from the fire outside, boys squabble happily in the dust.

November 10.
Arrangements, cables, provisions, lectures, briefings. We are travelling by lorry to a height of 14,000 feet in the Himalayas. I set out to buy ankle-length pants and lashings of woolies; return with two pairs of socks, an expensive water flask, the sort of scarf favoured by Victorian layabouts and a flute which cost 25 piastres. There is dire talk of frostbite, lung trouble and heart failure. If I'd stayed with the Standard Bank of South Africa I'd probably be a branch manager by now. A lecturer tells us that we shall meet members of the Monpa tribe. Savage war-cry from the British contingent of 'Monpa, Monpa, stick it up your jumper.'

10

November 11, 12, 13.

We assemble puffy-eyed and querulous at 4am. I wear underpants, swimming trunks, pyjamas, two pairs of trousers, two pairs of socks, sandboots, vest, shirt, two pullovers, scarf and Balaclava. I share a blue Japanese jeep with Anthony Mann, Tidmarsh, an Indian journalist and a little Japanese who peers from a padded anorak like a tortoise. We bounce through the paddy fields under cold stars arriving at Foothills at 6am.

Then off into the mountains with frequent stops for photographers to take pictures of hills and more hills. We sip Indian whisky and chew legs of sparrow-sized chicken. It is a matter of honour with our driver, a hard brown nut of a man, not to change down until the engine stalls on a hill with a 3,000 ft. drop beside us. The road was chiselled from the mountains in two years; from the depths of the valleys it looks like a fungoid root fed on the humus of eternity. Two hundred men are said to have died making it, plunging to the insect-singing jungle below or blowing themselves up with dynamite. We bump and labour through several strata — jungle, woodland with a golden bloom of autumn in it, pine forest watered by steel-blue streams, craggy highlands and finally sharp, starved peaks.

We pass refugee Monpa tribesmen pick-axing a road to their camp. They are woollen-booted, slant-eyed, ostensibly peaceful and gentle. They make prayer-like gestures of greeting. The children are plump and cheeky. Night falls bringing a false sense of security because we cannot see the precipices, just cushions of darkness, almost inviting. At last, 14 hours after leaving Tezpur, we arrive at our first base, Dirang.

We sleep on the stone floor of a bamboo billet and dine in the officers' mess off stew and rice, washed down with rum and hot water. At a briefing I ask an innocuous question and an emotional Indian journalist starts accusing the British Press of being anti-Indian. I tell him to be quiet but he becomes noisier and the briefing adjourns prematurely. I

11

return to the billet to find that someone has *borrowed* my sleeping bag. There is more noise and muted accusations; the Army finally provides me with another bag and I bed down after icy ablutions. We are at 6,000 feet.

On again at 4am to the Sela Pass which is 13,756 feet high. The camaraderie of mild hardship has grown up in our jeep. At 12,000 feet Tony Mann and I discuss Fleet Street personalities. Even the Jap's head emerges from his anorak. It is not too easy to breathe. Just before Sela Indian troops loose off a couple of 25-pounders for our benefit. I focus my camera unwaveringly on the wrong gun.

Sela is an iced and lonely place. Ten brisk steps and you've lost your breath. Through the fangs of the pass I can see the snow-capped peaks along which the disputed McMahon line was drawn. The Chinese are five miles away. The black-bearded Sikhs are fierce and friendly. They wear bracelets originally intended to accommodate the shaft of a broken sword or dagger. Nowadays they also use them as bottle openers.

In a hollow carpeted with alpine plants, leaves coated with gold dust, we eat lunch — lentil stew and tea. Altitude sickness strikes our Indian companion and we return to Dirang with him cossetted in blankets.

I am awoken at 5am by a jawan who gives me a marmalade sandwich and a cup of greasy tea. We drive, above a valley, to a temple on a plateau. Here the Abbot of Tawang, who fled from the Chinese, holds court for us. He is podgy, hairless, heavy-lidded and dignified. Tony Mann is presented with a scarf of butter muslin as the senior British Press member.

We tour the temple; lamas, all Monpas, in red sacking, recite prayers interminably and glance shyly at the camera-armed intruders. A band starts up, thumping drums and blasting ancient trumpets. We leave the monks to their seclusion, their beliefs, the benign care of Buddha and their band. I could stand almost everything except their band. Far below the river gushes past, boulders combing the water into white tresses.

12

We stop for breakfast at Bomdila. I guess the menu: lentils and tea. Twelve hours later we drop into the plains. A lot of hectic writing and captioning and then bed. I remove layers of trousers and pyjamas for the first time in three days. No one in the vicinity would doubt that I had been wearing them for a long time.

November 18.
Drew Pearson and I are invited for drinks at the home of two Italian-Indian women. We are asked to bring the drinks. They are in their forties and they worked in the padre's canteen for the RAF during the war — the great period of their lives. They tell jokes about Mae West and crease up with laughter; they also laugh uproariously at my jokes and I warm to them.

They live in white-washed poverty. They are big-boned, gaunt, the way I imagine Red Indian women to be like. Living with them is a grey-haired Anglo-Indian. He also collapses at my every sally, walloping the table and babbling, 'Sir . . . sir . . . oh, sir.' We leave beneath the stars by bicycle rickshaw.

November 19—23.
Time evaporates in a mêlée of impressions. First comes the news of a massive break-through by the Chinese. They out-flanked the Indian positions and cut the mountain road. In fact they must have been there when we drove through the hills.

Throughout the day fear fed by rumour sweeps the hot little town. From some journalists come a variety of reasons why they have to leave — no money left, no cameras, the impossibility of filing copy from Tezpur. One middle-aged American announces he will stay till the end. Then an Indian colonel looks into the club to announce: 'The last plane's leaving. Anyone who wants to can get on it. After that we take no responsibility for what happens to the Press.' The American drops his food and sprints to the waiting jeep.

About ten of us joined in the fellowship of danger, making

absurd jokes. Indian evacuees are leaving, the Chinese are said to be in the foothills.

We gather that if we spend the night with the new deputy commissioner – the old one has already fled – we may get away on the last bus and the last ferry across the Brahmaputra. We drink and smoke cigars on the verandah. From the direction of the fighting orange flares burst in the dark sky; beneath us the headlamps of lorries taking refugees to the river light the road.

We are awoken at 5am. The telephone to military HQ has gone dead: we must leave. We shovel our belongings on to an ancient bus and tour the town picking up the last engineer, the last jailer, the last everyone. There is a feeling of doom abroad, the morning light is clean and luminous. Outside the bank they are burning the money. One genius is also trying to burn the coins and beggars and children are grubbing in the red-hot ash for pickings.

A police officer dashes past in a comfortable car and orders a dozen armed police to get in our bus. With methodical madness they attempt to load bed-rolls, cooking pots and sacks of grain on the top of the sagging bus. We head for the river, picking up mothers and children, dropping bed-rolls and cooking pots.

The muddy beach is Dunkirk in miniature. Mississippi ferry boats trundle back and forth. Hill people are camped in the foreground, smoke from their fires coiling towards the pale sky; they cook fish netted from the opaque waters of the Brahmaputra and slit the throats of scrawny chickens. They are bewildered, resigned: this is their first taste of civilisation. Indians with bundles of belongings are scattered everywhere.

We listen to a transistor and hear for the first time that the Chinese have proposed a ceasefire. The suspicion that we have participated in an unseemly panic grows. Suddenly the beach reminds me of August Bank holiday at Southend – with the tide out.

In the evening I take a ferry with Terry Fincher, one of the best photographers in the business, to the other side. It is dusk; everywhere there is warm humanity, food cooking,

14

smoke, smouldering fires, looming dark faces, white teeth, an atmosphere of relief. Indians swarm around us asking where the Chinese are: others just stare and I cannot blame them because we bear two days' growth of beard and dirt to accompany it.

We manage to hire a jeep and rattle and bump to Nowgong, forty miles away. I file from a dusty telegraph office and in a restaurant renowned for its dysentery we drink tea — Nowgong is dry — and eat rice and chicken.

We meet some planters who have just sent their families to Calcutta and one offers us his house for the night. We enjoy the bliss of soft sheets, hot water, no mosquitoes. In the morning eggs and bacon! From a cinemascope window we see rhino grazing in the distance. Then back by jeep through the village of Jakhlabandha to the river. In the village I file again; as I leave the entire population is reading my cable. I wonder if any cable has reached London.

Back in Tezpur we realise the full extent of the panic. They have freed lunatics, convicts and the hospital patients. Shops are shuttered and the remaining townspeople are bitter at being deserted. In the club I open the fridge and find bad meat crawling with cockroaches as big as thumbs. We return to beans and sausages under siege by lunatics and convicts. But in conditions like this there is no one more reassuring than Terry Fincher, a Cockney who is as tough as a prize-fighter's knuckles when he's not convulsed with laughter.

November 24.
Terry and I decide in view of a cable breakdown to leave for Gauhati. Gauhati is civilisation after Tezpur. Here the same river looks broad and beautiful instead of flat and muddy. We book in at the Stadium Guest House. The town is the usual Indian bustle of gaudy silks, beggars, pharmacies, book shops. It is dry but we buy liquor and cheap cigars without difficulty. We buy some malaria preventatives, baggy underpants which tie up with tape and two porno-graphic paperbacks.

15

November 26.

We fly to Calcutta in a Fokker Friendship and are driven to the Grand Hotel by å large silent Sikh with another large silent Sikh beside him. The air is heavy with breathing, coughing and whimpering, as the pavement sleepers twitch and roll under their blankets. As we drive with suicidal intent through the suburbs white-clothed figures dart moth-like between the battling cars.

I have seen the beggars in Arab towns in Africa. They would be passed A1 fit for all duties compared with the beggars of Calcutta. One, with wizened legs, writhes along the pavement on his back with a money-pot perched on his navel; another, a hunch-backed dwarf, sidles along crabwise, hand outstretched. The children are armless, legless, scabbed, deformed.

November 29.

Back to Tezpur. The mosquitoes flutter out to meet me. On the way I meet Sid Williams from the *Daily Herald*, a likeable extrovert. On the plane he sits down and tears the trousers made up for him in Calcutta. He indicates this to the pigtailed air hostess who misunderstands his intentions. She maintains a haughty silence while Sid sits down again — and tears them even further with a noise like ripping calico.

December 1 and 2.

The story is played out now. The Chinese are honouring their promises to withdraw. There's a lot more quibbling to follow but, journalistically, nothing of interest. Three of us take a mattress on the grass and listen to the first Test.

December 3.

The Test on BBC World Service. The usual fighting recovery by England; ever since I heard my first Test I seem to have been listening to fighting recoveries. Sid Williams and I take a bicycle rickshaw down Tezpur's main street. A small, busy man on a new bicycle draws up beside us. Sid leans across and says: 'Where can we get a pineapple?' The cyclist explains that they're out of season. 'But I am getting you some,' he says. 'You see I am a policeman.' He arrives with four juicy pineapples and leaves with four rupees promising that he will find some more. I envisage our bedrooms stacked to the ceiling with pineapples before the week is out.

December 5.
It is 2.30pm and the afternoon sunshine is lambent. It is cool in my room; trees rustle and birds grumble. I remember scented evenings in Surrey, the breeze whispering in the leaves of a copper beech, dew on evening lawns, spangled rain from a lawn sprinkler. But my emotions deceive me because in England now it is grey and cold and children are gazing at heavy skies coaxing snow from them. In England, doubtless, I would be dreaming of white sands and warm seas.

December 6.
My last evening in Tezpur. I dine at the padre's, shake the hands of his old turbanned cook and tiny houseboy. Suddenly I become aware of their remoteness; we are parting as if we had just passed each other in the High Street. Our cycles have touched, withdrawn. I feel that the cycles were never meant to meet: that human folly momentarily overtook the pattern of things and brought us together.

December 8.
I drive for the last time through the Calcutta suburbs to the airport; through streets lined with cramped shops flaring with light like small hot caves, through saried and shirt-tailed hordes, through cows, goats, children, oxen, rickshaws, bicycles, through sweating layers of air spawning life, deformity, disease, poverty.

December 20.
I drive to Elstree to interview Richard Burton and Elizabeth

Taylor. For months their *friendship* has occupied endless columns of newspaper space. They are working on the set of a film called *The VIPs*. I always visualised Burton as a technicolour Hercules with Dylan Thomas's voice. He is short, greying-haired, courteous. Miss Taylor, of course, is late.

Burton, who has shared tumultuous screen passions with her in *Cleopatra*, seems vaguely embarrassed as he waits outside her studio caravan. She appears in a white two-piece, hair mounted in a cone; a small ordinary girl who pretends to decry the publicity that has helped make her famous. She has nice eyes: you might chat to her at a party where she would be among the six prettiest girls: you might not. The two of them are engulfed by photographers.

December 27.
The morning in Mitcham is electric blue. It strengthens into white purity. The snow that the children had begun to believe would never fall has fallen. You can sense it before you draw the curtains. The thin garden behind our new end-terrace is a white pasture: the weeping willow in the front patch is sheathed in frozen tears. The snow is six inches deep, Christmas card, old-fashioned stuff, still falling.

Breakfast is wolfed down, bacon crisper than ever before, coffee hotter and stronger. Already the children are outside. Phantom snowmen arise in the falling flakes, snowballs fly, small children cry thinly in the muffled air as missiles mittened into ice strike them on wind-cherried ears. Mufflers steam, fingers ache. I walk to the bus-stop holding with bravado a rainbow golf umbrella. A snow-ball plops on my canopy of many colours, snow-bandaged giggles follow me into the frozen haze. There is no dignity today unless you possess coal nugget eyes and smoke a sagging pipe.

December 30.
It has snowed again overnight. The snow is a foot deep now and Sunday morning is full of children's voices. Patrick and the boy next door build a seven-foot snowman; men who

18

clatter lawnmowers all summer scrape their garden paths and curse happily; dogs snout and scuffle but cats are still pussy-prim. Twigs bend under wedges of snow, starlings cluster in high branches, breasts pouting, chatter frozen.

I walk to the station across a desolate park as the mauve shadows fill the folds and crevasses, embrace the stillness and the silence and the loneliness. All that is missing is a man taking his dog for a walk. It is the worst — or best — snowfall for years: it was last year and the year before and it will be next year. Britons are aghast at the chaos caused by the snow: as they were last year and the year before, as they will be next year. In the Congo they are fighting again: as they were last year and most probably will be next year, which is the day after tomorrow.

1963

January 9.

Another mixed bag. In the morning two inquests at Battersea. A woman who set herself ablaze lighting a cigarette and two children gassed in a basement flat. The mother of the children is twenty, a tiny, whispering girl in a huge green coat and a black net scarf. She is taut with grief but refuses to leave the court while a pathologist gives the sickening details of death.

All coroners' courts are the same − dull walls, avuncular coroners, stolid police officers, huddles of witnesses bewildered that this could happen to them. They wear stained raincoats, black ties, Marks and Spencer headscarves. The deaths of the rich rarely reach these hopeless places. This coroner is benign, boyish and ready with stock phrases of sympathy. One of the children, it materialises, switched on the gas fire while the mother was upstairs. Accidental death.

In the evening I drive to Mill Hill to interview champion driver Graham Hill with his wife and two children. He is brown-eyed, moustached, long-faced. I look in vain for evidence of the devil-may-care attitude that one would expect from a man who hurtles round Grand Prix circuits at more than 100 m.p.h. He looks like a prosperous salesman who plays golf at the weekend. In another era he would probably have occupied himself shooting German bombers out of summer skies. He has no thought of retirement. His wife tells me: 'We Grand Prix wives do not think about the dangers − I suppose we shut it out of our minds.' Unfortunately the Graham Hill/Mill Hill coincidence confuses me and when I phone the story I call him Phil Hill, another racing driver. Later I babble a correction over the phone but a sub-editor, so often the saviour of the reporter, has juggled the Hills. What will happen if I interview Phil Hill? Ever heard of a driver called Mill Hill?

January 18.
Gaitskell dies. I drive through iced suburbs, flurried with snow, to ask George Brown for his comments. He is not at home. It is a cruel night to die. I stop at a pub in Herne Hill to seek warmth and humanity. The men and women who might have made him Prime Minister talk about everything except his death. Perhaps they don't know. I experience a sudden attachment to socialist ideals as I drive past terraced houses, ordinary pubs, newsagents, the occasional lonely figure becalmed in the frozen night. This is the soiled brick and brown-paint heart of Gaitskell's world of equality − where most of them probably voted Tory.

There was a quickening of reflexes in the office when the news broke but no panic because his death had been anticipated. In go the prepared pages, quotes mouthed while his heart still beat. Nonetheless not without sincerity. In our little Fleet Street pub known as Poppins the power has failed and our faces are lit by gaslight and candles. It has been a strange, lonely night, dusted with snow, and haunted by the crumpled face of a leader who always seemed unfulfilled.

January 26.
I take the family to Alexandra Palace where I once played as a child. It is the most splendidly ugly building I have ever seen − far uglier than the Albert Memorial but without the uncompromising ugliness of modern skyscrapers. It looms over North London, an elephantine grey barracks domed with dirty glass standing on a grass-sloped hill above a racecourse. It has in its time housed the largest organ in

22

Europe, a multitude of exhibitions, German prisoners in World War I, Maltese refugees in World War II. It was built in 1873 and burned down; rebuilt in 1875 as North London's answer to the Crystal Palace.

When I was a child it was in disuse and we used to roam its high corridors lined in places with slot machines — girls with cupid-bow lips taking off their clothes with erratic abandon, pistols that knocked metal cats off their perches with lead pellets, cranes that grabbed and dropped mildewed trinkets. We crept stealthily into a vast hall where pigeons flapped through the rafters and hollow music played by an unseen organist issued from Wagnerian ranks of pipes; we sniffed the unmistakable smell of the Ally Pally — rusty, beery, decayed.

They have since tried to modernise it with a restaurant and a bar, but no one can really change this superb monstrosity: it is too big, too ugly, too much itself. I peer through the keyhole of a locked door and catch a whiff of liquor splashed fifty years ago, trapped organ music, pigeon droppings and dead rats.

Outside children toboggan on the gentle slopes covered with melting snow; the lake where the little paddle boats bob around an island is frozen solid; the football pitch where my father and I watched Alexandra Palace play — they had a young Matthews of a winger in those days — is a foot deep in snow.

On the way back we stop outside my old home, a mansion that has shrunk to a doll's house. The great buttercup field at the end of the road is a handkerchief. I see a short, smart man leave the house with a leggy boy at his side: they turn and head towards the Palace, the cricket and football, and disappear, contented and secure in their long-ago dimension. I awake and notice that the leggy boy beside me, Patrick, is a replica of that other boy — all trust and eagerness and wanting-to-know. We drive back through the snow to our own house, our own time.

January 30.
A Soho day digging out background on two thugs shot dead the previous evening. Call at the usual pubs, strip clubs, clip joints. Climb the stairs to one clip joint and find four dirty girls huddled round an electric fire. It is the girls' job to entice the naive into buying non-alcoholic drinks at 10s. a time. You would have to be naive to the point of simple-mindedness to consider buying them a cup of tea. The shooting was in a club called The Bus Stop. The manager, Melvin, shot the owner, Tony Mella, three times and then turned the gun on himself. They were lifelong friends. Happily the shooting was two doors from the Yorkminster, a pleasant enough pub where you can sit back with a beer or a Pernod and observe queers, crooks, literary eccentrics, all sizes of leather jackets, jeans and black stockings, pretty girls with dank hair and flour-pale faces. They say Soho is a quaint village stolen from Bohemia: give me Brixton High Street on a wet Saturday afternoon any day.

January 31.
A £50 emerald is missing from the Crown jewels. Spend the day looking for the people looking for it. In the course of my search I meet Tim Carew, author, journalist, ex-Gurkha and humourist. He has a delayed laugh so that you have to wait a second or two before *your* joke is appreciated. This usually occurs when he has sunk his head into a pint of bitter and the result is explosive, foamy and wet.

I tell him how a typist once took it upon herself to change some of the expletives in an unpublished short story I wrote. When the manuscript returned a villain who exclaimed 'Bloody hell' was heard to mutter 'Oh, my hat'. We decided to abandon obscene oaths for the day and to restrain ourselves to 'Golly gumdrops, Ye Gods, good grief and odds fish'. After some experimental exchanges we notice people drifting away from us. Fail to find the emerald hunters.

February 8.
Dagenham, Essex. A foggy night washed with drizzle, soiled

snow piled in the gutters. I walk past the hulk of Fords, blazing with workshop lights, smouldering with strikes, to a hall, draughty and comtemporary. George Brown, Wilson's rival for leadership of the Labour Party, is to speak. Apathy overwhelms me as the audience assembles — trade unionists, suburban idealists, bitter ageing men, lots of thick scarves and silent approbation of the warm-up platitudes. One speaker whines back to the unemployment of the '20s. A young adenoidal schoolmaster invokes class warfare.

Brown, smooth but uninspiring, concentrates on unemployment, the failure of the Common Market talks and some anti-Tory invective. Even his insults lack bite. It depresses me to see the ideals of socialism reduced to drab conformity by such a gathering as this. The losses to the Labour Party of Bevan and Gaitskell suddenly seem irreplaceable. The meeting has a predictable effect on my shifty politics: it makes me a Tory again. Only one event could re-convert me to socialism: a meeting of fanatical Tories. There's nothing like an audience of smug-bonneted women applauding the rehearsed drolleries of a Cabinet Minister to put you on the road to communism.

February 14.
Transport House for Press conference given by Harold Wilson 45 minutes after announcement that he has beaten George Brown for leadership of the Labour Party. The hall is packed with political correspondents and jostling photographers, harsh with the glare of TV floodlights. There is something faintly unseemly about this public airing of the personality cult in a movement founded on poverty and idealism. That's the way it has to be but on this showing Wilson doesn't possess the presence of a leader. He is short and nasal, employs a destructive wit and is studiously self-effacing about his success. None of this adds up to leadership, though, and I don't fancy his chances in a diplomatic clash with Kruschev or Kennedy. There was a dour kernel of sincerity that served as a substitute for Churchillian flamboyance in Attlee, a superb disregard for

the mouthings of lesser beings displayed by that Edwardian squire, Macmillan, that passes for authority. Wilson has yet to show some quality that will expand his personality beyond the walls of the House of Commons into the wide open spaces of world statesmanship.

February 15.
A true blue evening for a change. Macmillan at a Tory dinner in Bromley. Tables lined with dinner jackets and half-bared bosoms. Turkey and peach melba, of course; brandy and desiccated cigars for the speeches.

Macmillan is his usual droll self: he stirs his familiar cocktail — jingoism, a call to youth, with a dash of mild humour delivered with theatrical timing. One admires his professionalism, deprecates his patronising air. Local Tories usually knock over the brandy in their eagerness to bellow the first 'Hear, hear'; this bunch do not fawn with such enthusiasm. Behind the tooled rhetoric I sense alarm and despondency as he refers to the faint-hearts, i.e. critics of the Common Market fiasco. But for all his affectation he is the only politician of the moment with the assurance and personality of leadership.

February 19.
I interview a twentieth century diarist who must rank alongside Pepys and William Hickey — Mrs Dale. The actress, Ellis Powell, has just been fired from the radio serial. I have evaded the trivialities that she has intoned for 15 years: now she is leaving I feel sorry. She bridged two decades and became one of the fittings of an era — homely and dull but as much a part of 7 million homes as the radio itself.

She downs a double gin and talks bitterly about her treatment by the BBC. Happily her character bears no relation to Mrs Dale — she is jovial, actressy, sensible. I was surprised to learn she only earned £25 a week: she also has a healthy disrespect for Mrs Dale. After 15 years I should have thought she would have assimilated some of the

26

personality of her radio image: there is no resemblance to Mrs D. whatsoever.

February 20.
I take a taxi to Old Street Court for top civil servant accused of importuning. The case is adjourned and I walk back through the City that is stirring in the touch of the first sunshine for months; its still-cold fingers find mellow colours in old churches hiding between hulking new office blocks and stains of fawn, rust and ochre between icicles of soot. I discover a second-hand book shop specialising in cricket books — a restful, musty place where you can flick pages and relight days of majestic tranquillity at Lord's or the Oval; close your eyes and see top-hatted batsmen with mutton-chop whiskers elegantly driving with bow-shaped bats; hear the imprecations of W.G. Grace, the rustle of genteel applause on a summer breeze; transport yourself to a village green with a tankard in your hand.

February 22.
On a train to Canterbury. The countryside twirling past is slowly melting in this first sunshine. The fields are still white sheets stitched with hedges but furrows of earth are now showing where the frozen nap has worn thin. It is bare and beautiful; an aloof stranger beginning to thaw and beckon. I want to leap from the train and walk up a hillside patched with fields, breathe the melting air.

Canterbury has not yet made up its mind what to be — a new town or an ancient centre of tourism. Its task is complicated by the melding of old and new architecture after the bombing in the last war.

Today's story: street warfare between local boys and pupils from King's School. The King's boys have to wear straw boaters and some of them carry canes; the warfare is therefore a calculated risk on the part of the King's School authorities. The only mystery is why it hasn't broken out before. The uniform is a tradition with which they could well dispense for the sake of decorum but, of course, the *uniform* of the local partisans — winkle-picker shoes, skin-tight jeans; bunched quiffs — is just as bizarre.

Later I have a drink with Norman Potter, photographer, friend and accomplice, in a garish club in Streatham, decorated like a South Sea islands bar. We meet a retired boxer and his hearty blonde wife who loves and loathes him. He speaks with the nasal intonation that is one of the hallmarks of the pugilist whose nose has been pulverised incessantly. 'He gets on my goat,' she says, 'when all the young girls come up and ask him how he is.' Enigmatic smile from pugilist. 'I wouldn't mind so much if he admitted knowing them.' He rubs knuckle-flattened nose reflectively. 'But he won't — always says he's never seen any of them before — bloody liar.' As she works herself up the middle-aged boxer retires into blood-stained memories. 'He's always been one for the birds — wish I'd never met him sometimes.' She smiles heroically. 'But he's lovely really, a proper gent.' 'What are you having, duck?' the proper gent enquires.

March 16.
An early morning start to ask War Minister John Profumo about his reported offer to resign over the Christine Keeler allegations. Lots of traffic and parking problems. I finally park on top of a large white NO PARKING sign outside his house, a yellow tomb of a place behind the Nash terraces at Regent's Park. He emerges and climbs into a black saloon clutching two dispatch boxes. He is smallish, too dapper, velvet collar on his black coat, polite and pleasant. 'Absolutely no truth in it,' he says. How many times have I been told that when there is all the truth in the world in it? He returns and departs again with his wife, former actress Valerie Hobson, aloof and ministerial in a brick-red two piece.

March 17.
Off to the new skyscraper London Hilton Hotel in Park Lane. Work on the building has been held up and there is a

28

staff of 700 attending 17 guests who decided to come, despite the inconvenience. Page-boys with no one to page, phone booths with no phones, bundles of rainbow-coloured wires hanging in bunches, a stone polisher polishing stone.

A woman PRO informs me that I can't possibly write a story until the Press reception in a few weeks' time. This determines me to write a story. I find the first guest, the wife of an American accountant, and interview her in the glacial foyer while an under-manager fumes nearby. She speaks with a soft drawl, loves the hotel — especially the iced water in the taps — and everything about it because it's just like home. She then admits she's a Londoner who married an American nine years ago. Her love for the new hotel, she says, has nothing to do with the fact that her husband is an employee here.

March 18.
Catch 1.35am plane for Geneva en route to Zermatt where a typhoid epidemic has broken out. I meet a tall, soft-spoken blonde at London Airport but forget where I have met her before. Then my memory stirs: she is Joan Rhodes, the girl who bends iron bars and tears phone books in half for a living. I last met her in Nairobi where she was in cabaret. She is on her way to do a one-night stand in Geneva. She is one of the gentlest persons I have met. She chuckles with good humour but there is something sad about her. I can imagine the inevitable jokes and defensive attitudes of most men. We part at Geneva and she walks off carrying her iron bars as if they were matchsticks.

On the train to Zermatt I meet a young man from Leeds and his girl friend — a Tiller girl whom I must have seen on television. We go as far as Visp together, making tourist jokes about money, food and breaking our legs when we ski.

The train trundles on to Zermatt, through pine-stilted slopes and ever-thickening snow. The town is shrouded with mist; it is the usual ski resort complete with boutiques selling jumpers and curios, healthy-looking men and sleek women. Even the sick look healthy with their shoe-polish tans. The

Swiss are trying to play down the epidemic: their euphemisms are not impressive and I file as many of the facts as I can find out. The restaurants and bars are packed with young things from France, Germany, Italy and Britain. They eat and drink a lot and dance slowly and thoughtfully in tight ski-pants and steaming sweaters, heading towards bed in fox-trot rhythm.

March 19.
Awoken by blue and gold light flooding my room. I look out at brilliant white peaks cutting the sky. It is a glittering day full of energy but lacking the expectancy of an English spring day. I breakfast on chocolate — wouldn't touch the stuff at home — and rolls. Stroll around the village but the expensive clothes and complexions do not compare favourably with the raw white beauty above them.

There are as many typhoid rumours in the Alps as there were Chinese rumours in the Himalayas. If only some of these people could have experienced a little hardship: I can never forget the disparity of classes: I sip a beer among a lot of gossip-column accents and remember my Essex Socialists with their dull, determined minds. I tuck away class thoughts with ease and tuck into a chicken dinner.

March 20.
No wonder they have typhoid. I wander behind the wooden chalets ostensibly pure and clean in their snow-jackets and find a stream littered with garbage. The pristine myth of Switzerland's cleanliness has melted. Once tourists looked at such a stream and found it quaint: now they will find it disgusting. Once they listened to the cow-bells in the mountains and smiled with predictable pleasure: now they will point out the cows' cramped and dirty quarters.

Businessmen are understandably worried by the epidemic because it hits them where it hurts most, in their pockets. Many tourists believe the typhoid outbreak was hushed up in its early stages to avoid damaging the tourist trade. An English doctor tells me: 'I was appalled by the lack of precautions to stop the epidemic spreading. Behind the façade of cleanliness there is utter filth.' So much for those healthy tans and antiseptic hotels.

I catch the mountain train to Brig. A middle-aged woman in purple stockings and fur jacket sits opposite me, revealing generous lengths of purple hose, and frowns at the mountains. I label her bad-tempered French or Italian. Her husband arrives and she speaks with a New York drawl. They row in a surly way and she announces: 'I am not, positively not, carrying any cases.' Her husband, a Swiss, shrugs his shoulders, and returns to another part of the train. She discloses a few more purple inches and scowls with renewed hatred at the crags and ravines. I am not sorry to leave the tans, cups of chocolate, thick-crusted snow, the wealthy with their self-indulgent ski-clothes and hair styles, legs in plaster casts, the expensive beer, the concealed dirt, the typhoid.

Stay the night in the Hotel Regina on Geneva's lakeside. More comfortable and homely than anything Zermatt had to offer. Look into a club for a drink. Lots of beautiful girls with lacquered hair taking their clothes off. Paradoxically there is something sexless about them. They giggle and fawn and only react to the crackle of paper money, bar girls the world over.

March 21.
A few hours to kill before catching the London plane. Geneva is a broad, comfortable city happily blending the old and new. Across the lake all the buildings look like the Grand Hotel, Brighton. Or Eastbourne sea-front. In Britain they would have filled in part of the lake by now and made it into a car park. Fly back in a Comet and land, pleased as always, to be back in London. Final reflection on Switzerland: while I was mixing with the sleekly rich dining off steaks and escargots it was Freedom from Hunger Week.

March 26.
Profumo makes a statement in the House of Commons

31

about the rumours linking his name with the missing witness in an Old Bailey trial, Christine Keeler. He denies the rumours, says he last met Miss Keeler in 1961 with his wife, Valerie Hobson, and threatens legal action if rumours are repeated in any way. I resume my place outside his house but am recalled after half an hour to cover the death of property magnate Walter Flack. He built an empire on a £300 Army gratuity and was found dead in his bath at Whitehall Court, a block he bought for £1 million. Rich or poor you're a long time dead.

March 27.
Three spells of late shifts, 9.30pm—4.30am. The all-night buses are full of regulars — printers, club girls, drunks, West End revellers, flash-suited West Indians, Italian waiters, beggars and thugs. I wait for the bus beside an embankment stall that sells saccharine-sweet tea and cheese rolls. Sparks from a brazier stuffed with blazing wood spiral into the darkness and old men with ruined faces hold rambling conversations with themselves: old harridans solicit; ratty youths pick pockets; across the street the river slides past on its molten silver trail to the sea.

The passengers on the bus are matey and jocular, sharing night-time camaraderie. Once I saw a huge West Indian pass a hefty printer a note. There was an explosion of anger from the printer and the West Indian skipped off the bus. 'I don't mind nig-nogs and I don't mind queers,' the printer said. 'But I do object to nig-nog queers. That's reasonable, isn't it?' Apparently the note read: 'I love you.'

I arrive home as a faint blue light pierces the bruise-coloured clouds. As I stand in the small back garden I smell the warm yeasty breath from the nearby bakery. I go to bed but cannot sleep; I am not a true night person.

March 28.
Cambridge dons have protested at recommendation to give Lord Hailsham an honorary degree. They are angered by his comments that America pinches our scientists to shore up

inadequacies in its educational system. I drive to Folkstone to see Hailsham, who is speaking at a young Tory conference. I stop at a pub full of birds at Charing. Bright-feathered birds thousands of miles from their jungles squawk in bizarre domesticity; sabre-beaked parrots bob, bow and blink bare eyes.

Meet Hailsham in the lounge of the Burlington Hotel. He is munching fragments of afternoon tea with two young female Tories. 'Do you alter your statement one iota?' I ask. 'I don't know,' he says, 'I didn't put any iotas in it.' This sally ignites happy twittering from the young Tories, powdery, bonneted and blue.

Hailsham is jocular, intelligent, mildly eccentric. Much of the eccentricity is deliberate – boots, beach-bathing, bell-ringing – and has probably deprived him of the chance of vying for leadership of the Tory party. 'Make sure you spell my name correctly,' says the earnest young Tory chairman. 'I will,' I say, making note not to mention his name at all.

It is a gusty, exhilarating day with a salt-and-sunshine wind bowling along the cliffs. There are two levels of Folkstone: the upper crust on the cliffs where retired gentlefolk live gentle lives and nannies rebuke sailor-suited children, and the lower crust where cross-channel ferries steam from the quayside and café owners stare glumly at the decaying, wind-blown desolation around them.

Lord Hailsham makes political history by taking his dog Jones on the electoral platform with him. 'I had to bring him,' he tells me. 'He looked so unhappy when he thought I was going without him.' Jones, a three-year-old Welsh springer, folds himself beneath a Union Jack. 'This is most unusual,' mutters the nameless young Tory chairman. Half way through the speech-making Jones is given a drink of water in an ash tray; he has been trained to paw the party line.

March 31.
To the Palladium following up a story about one of the showbiz football teams. During rehearsal for tonight's show

I wait at the stage door where I once lay in wait in another age of journalism. In those days it was news if a TV personality sneezed. But trends subtly change: that was also the era of Gretna Green elopements, pop-singers' hysterics and gang warfare. Today a Gretna Green marriage hardly rates a paragraph. There have been interim phases: race riots had a six-month run, Trafalgar Square sit-down demonstrations lasted well: today a minor mutiny in the Army merits a lot of column inches but will pass unnoticed by the autumn. A galaxy of personalities has risen and subsided: once Lady Docker only had to complain about the hors d'oeuvre at a Mayfair restaurant to make a page lead; Lady Barnett, Barbara Kelly (I once had to ask her if she thought she had knobbly knees), Dickie Valentine, Billy Hill, Jack Spot, Lady Lewisham, Michael Parker . . . they all studded the pages in their periods; some still operate in their respective fields but no longer make news. The late Gilbert Harding, who duped the public into believing that rudeness plus erudition equalled wit, was always good for a story.

Through the swing doors emerge the Tiller girl and her boy friend whom I met on the way to Zermatt. They are brown and happy together. Millicent Martin, pert and twangy-voiced, appears and we adjourn to their dressing room where the influence of Jimmy Edwards is apparent in the furnishings — a couch and a barrel of beer. Millicent Martin, who was satirizing smart-set girls and women reporters on TV the previous night, is an ordinary, pretty little thing. Why are we always so surprised when stars turn out to be ordinary with two eyes and ears and ingrowing toenails? The satirists are successful because they ridicule the successful, popular targets. One of the best targets for satire would surely be satirists. Conversation with Miss Martin proceeds along these lines: 'Oh, I do feel tired this morning.' 'Do you?' 'Yes, — I was up till three this morning.' 'It's the extra hour for summer-time.' 'Yes, I suppose it is — oh, I do feel tired.'

Spend the afternoon with Jimmy Edwards at the Victoria Palace. He is rehearsing a brass band concert for the Young Brass Band Association in the evening. The empty theatre is pickled in laughter after years of Crazy Gang nights: double-takes, female impersonations, custard pies, jokes as ripe as Stilton.

Mr Edwards, prospective Tory candidate for Paddington North, goes through his act with tuba, euphonium and trombone which I once saw him perform at the Windmill. He confides that he takes brass bands seriously and once blew for Barnes Borough. He conducts three bands — 'This bit is serious and if I fall off the rostrum it's an accident' — and the old theatre swells with rich, thumping music.

April 1.
Thorpe Bay, sedate sister of slap-happy Southend. Fat comfortable houses, all roads leading to the Thames estuary promenade. The mood of the waterfront is variable: sometimes blustery with salt-sea buoyancy, sometimes placid with river tranquillity. As the promenade. approaches Southend, winkle stalls and ice-cream parlours take over.

I want to interview Olga Dawson, wife of Cockney financier George Dawson, whose marriage was dissolved today. A foreign maid tells me she is away for a couple of days: I do not believe her. A taxi pulls in behind the office car; the occupant glances at us, the taxi drives off. It is obviously Olga Dawson, despite more denials from the loyal maid. I suspect that she will go to the nearest pub, have a quiet drink and wait for me to leave. This is exactly what she does do and I find her in the Halfway House. She has a sad, refined face. She is reticent, friendly and worried about the health of their youngest child. George still visits her to see the children. I have a feeling that they should have stayed together, but it is none of my business.

April 2.
Back to Southend to interview the Chief Constable about a

35

shop-lifting case being debated in the House of Lords. While I was on the train to Southend he was proceeding towards London.

Have a drink in a cellar club with a text-book Irish thief, full of blarney and beer. He is 39 with hard good looks, sleek hair, hawkish face. He claims to be a friend of Jack Doyle and is proud of a recent £30 fine for stealing an overcoat from a pub. He chats cheerfully about allegations that he has been stealing roast chickens from a pub, lowering them from a window on to a ledge outside the gents and collecting them there. He is upset that the pub has now barred him. Together we visit a few pubs and meet a few characters living on their wits and the dole. But soon the seediness and swearing become boring. I take a last look across the fish-wet, mud straits, the endless pier and the promenade shrubberies and go home.

April 8.
Garrards, the jewellers, on a fine spring morning. I sidle in with a photographer — you can't stride into Garrards — in search of a story about a soldier who went there to learn how to shine his buttons and badges. Showcases glitter with diamond eyes and the sunshine lights fires of gold. Shop assistants cat-pad about on grey carpets appraising customers: they don't fawn, they don't patronise but they pigeon-hole you all right — gentry, nouveau riche, criminal, impoverished-but-curious.

We see a pale department head wearing a funereal dark suit. 'Why do you want to know this?' he enquires, just managing to restrain his outrage. We tell him. 'Really,' pettishly, 'this is a private matter between us and the Army.', Story confirmed! Obviously he thinks we are thieves. He introduces us to a floor director and retires as self-effacingly as his tight suit will allow.

The director is reasonable, helpful, cautious. I lean on a showcase, noting that it contains a diamond necklace priced at £935. We leave this haven of muted suspicion and crystalline elegance and breathe the sun-warmed, petrol-pungent air of Regent Street.

April 16.
Easter Monday. I have taken the family to my parents' house in Torquay and we join the crowds at Paignton Zoo where the animals are expecting us. It wouldn't be a Bank Holiday if we weren't there for their delectation. As we pour through the gates they move to vantage points — gibbons swinging across trees, ducks with unblinking eyes propelling themselves to the shallows, elephants unpacking their trunks, bears sheathing their talons and squatting on their haunches. This year a fine collection of specimens, exotic and domestic, has been assembled in the drizzle for them — girls with high-sprung hair sagging in the rain and orange rinses staining their necks; youths in stocking-tight jeans ducking the rain-drops ski-ing down duck-styled lubricated hair and shying peanuts at girls hovering between unattainable dignity and giggling surrender; bowed fathers and flushed mothers calling their children in monkey row; wellington-booted, munching children feeding buns to the bears.

The monkeys get the best view of the steaming, crumpled visitors from the smooth branches of long-dead trees. The specimens gibber and point, bare their teeth, suck spluttering wet pipes, cuff their children, emit lemonade belches, poke stale cake through the bars and scratch themselves.

The younger exhibits display themselves on the Jungle Express which circles a pond while their parents go to the feeding houses for tea, crisps and individual pies.

Elephants lean leather necks on the fence and take buns in their trunks because it encourages the visitors to stay; big cats appraise lazily from their straw beds; badgers and foxes patrol their bars, anxious not to miss a specimen or a pink hand stretching out to be bitten.

In the bird house parrots and parakeets side-step along their perches to stare with yellow-button eyes, cocking

37

crested heads to hear the calls of the visitors. Blossom-headed parakeets, masked lovebirds, blue and red macaws bend to persuade children to cluck and whistle — if a bird is very patient he can make a child cluck like a parrot. Only the Festive Parrot looks glum and refuses to train anyone.

Dusk and drizzle thicken, a penguin waves, a gibbon falls from the stands. The gates close; the show is over.

April 17.
A choppy, salty day in Torquay. The wind tosses showers of saline rain into the hills, studded with grey and white mansions, and the traffic-choked main street below. The big houses recall an era of comfortable elegance — comfortable, that is, for the few, not quite so comfortable for those in the cramped terraces jostling each other in the shade of the hills. Now builders are destroying the town's mellow profile with skyscraper blocks of flats. Local architects probably shudder at the factory chimneys of the north; blinded by the prospect of fat rents among the palm trees they can't perceive the ugliness of their luxury tenements.

We walk round the harbour, where dinghies and yachts and swans dragging black-paddle feet are moored, and call at an amusement arcade where the law now permits you to lose money at games of chance where you have no chance.

April 18.
Dartmoor with wind-driven April showers showering tors and crags, sodden bracken and heather. I rinse my face in the rain and swallow a gust of wind. The wind switches the tails and manes of inquisitive ponies and drives sheep and lambs with dainty feet into the shelter of old stone walls. Roads have brought picnic civilization to the moors but there is still wild, brooding beauty on the bracken-brown heights.

We stop at Princetown with its granite-ugly gaol and even uglier houses. It is difficult to imagine that so many hard, hopeless men are imprisoned in the grey barns of the prison. If I met a prisoner fleeing across the moor I doubt if I would give him away. But what if he had been imprisoned for assaulting a child or beating up an old woman?

April 21.
Angus Ogilvy, who marries Princess Alexandra on Wednesday, has had an accident in his new Mark 10 Jaguar. Apparently he pulled up sharply at a zebra crossing and ground the aristocratic nose of the Jag into the rear of a Mini. No one was hurt and the accident probably further endeared him to the public. He and his fiancée are currently spokes in the Royal wheel. They have a cheerful disregard for protocol and get involved in the sort of mishaps that occur to all of us. I hope neither is spoiled by enforced snobbery. They could be Britain's finest ambassadors. I spend the evening looking for the driver of the Mini: I fail.

April 24.
A day at the races. I arrive early at Epsom Downs to find tensions muted and buffered by mist. I remember the days when, icy-limbed and aching-lunged, I took part in cross-country runs from Epsom College, past the empty grandstand and the green river of the racecourse. If we were caught at the Derby we were expelled.

Today I join Norman Martlew of Littlewoods, formerly of the *Daily Mirror*, in a grandstand box. There is cold turkey and salmon for lunch, and we privileged guests enjoy panoramic views of the Downs, the pigmy punters and bookies beneath. Seven journalists run a syndicate, 35s a race, and lose steadily throughout the afternoon. But the feel of the racecourse is missing in this expensive gallery.

I go down near the rails and meet Albert Dimes, an East End bookie. 'What have you done in the next race?' he asks. I say nothing and he says, 'Easy to Love — get on while the price is right.' I get on at 6—1 and see Easy to Love easily beaten into fourth place. You can't see the finish down here but you are right beside the thundering, sweating excitement of the race: the crouching, whipping jockeys in their bright silks, the beautiful animals with staring eyes and straining sinews, the chanting of the crowd as the favourite comes up on the outside.

I manage to recoup the sydicate's losses on the last race, picking up £9.4s. on the favourite, Queen's Copper. I am very popular. We journalists leave the Downs with its hangover of lost hope and screwed-up betting tickets and drive to the Marquis of Granby in Epsom for a few drinks from the winnings. I meet a middle-aged man with silver hair who could be a bookie or a vicar. I ask him if he is a bookie and he says he is a detective from Bow Street. He has just arrested a group of Cypriots trying to work the three card trick.

April 27.
A lazy dewy Saturday morning. The sky is hazy and latent with the first heat of the year. Suddenly trees have unwrapped pale green leaves and streets of semi-detacheds are clouded with cumulus of almond and cherry blossom. Our cat, Barnaby, stretches and nuzzles the mint; first lawnmowers clatter and neighbours come outdoors to listen to the radio indoors. Smitten with gambling fever I take the family to Sandown Park. Patrick and Martin are given free race cards and pencils and the flamboyant tipster Prince Monolulu speaks to Martin, aged 6, who is deeply impressed. We sit by the rails among picnicking punters. The sun is hot and the lollies melt and girls in tights and black boots stretch out languorously while their escorts study form and hard humourless men fan themselves with race cards and roll greasy cigarettes.

One race is over the sticks and an injured horse owned by Gregory Peck, named Owen Sedge, has to be shot. I remark to a track official that shooting these animals when they are no longer able to win races is a sad reflection on the Sport of Kings. To my surprise he agrees with me. There is probably justification in this case but not in others: it is often merely that it would cost the horse-lovers too much money to pay the medical bills. The death of the animal struggling to leap the fences for reasons which it probably never understood sours the sun-glazed afternoon.

April 29.
A five-week-old baby snatched from a pram in Muswell Hill
where I was born. I arrive to find baby has been found. It
was *borrowed* by two schoolgirl sisters who walked with it
for two miles after hearing it crying in its pram. The mother,
aged 36, cradles the baby in a kitchen crowded with
neighbours and nappies and talks about her ordeal. 'I
regretted every time I had been cross with him when he cried
at night,' she says. 'He has never seemed so precious as he
did when he was gone.' The tiny baby, born prematurely,
opens periwinkle eyes and breaks wind.

May 2.
Sir Winston Churchill has announced that he will not seek
re-election as Woodford's MP at the next election. I go to
Woodford to assess reaction. The centre of the constituency
is green, comfortable and politically lethargic because it has
been the safest of safe seats for so long.

The Tory HQ consists of one room at the back of a
Victorian house. A vague, pleasant young woman says: 'I
don't really know much about what's going on — I only
come in a few times a week.' The postman does know what's
going on. He prophesies that a Liberal will win the next
election.

A bronze statue of Churchill broods majestically across
the passing traffic while an old woman with fluttering hands
and beaming spectacles snips the withered heads of daffodils
in a nearby garden. She says: 'I wish they would look after
the statue. I get so angry when boys snowball it. And when
Sir Winston broke his leg they put a newspaper splint round
the bronze leg.'

Sitting in the office car I hear that Ellis Powell, alias Mrs
Dale, has died in the Temperance Hospital from a cerebral
haemorrhage. It requires concentration to assimilate the
death of someone who was so recently alive in your presence.
But there is no time to mourn: I drive to the White House,
where Sir Winston used to stay with Col. Sir Stuart Mallinson.

41

I find myself in an oasis of gracious living. A mellow house, alive with photographs of Churchhill, panelled in delicately-grained woods. Sir Stuart enthusiastically pilots me round his exhibits – in the garden a red oak sapling thickening into manhood that was planted by Churchill, a diary kept by Churchill, a bronze bust of him lit by a spotlight. The study is panelled in wood collected from the battlefield of Ypres.

May 3.
Dispatched to the Bankruptcy Court where broken dreams, scuttled fortunes, lost ambitions and fat frauds are distilled into chilling debits. The corridors are tall and reproving, the men who work there hardened to human frailty.

Actor Bruce Seton, who played Fabian in a TV detective series, seeks and gets his discharge from bankruptcy. He blames type-casting – the nightmare of television actors – for his failure. Recent ill health is mentioned in court. Outside the court Seton says: 'Anyone would have thought I'd had a nasty cold – in fact I've just had a lung removed.' He has just inherited a title and is now Sir Bruce Seton of Abercorn. Motto 'Onward Ours'. He talks in a breathless voice; he has kind eyes and severe good looks eroded by his recent illness.

Back at the office I unearth the envelope of Seton cuttings that trace his life, success and failure. A young man with Sandhurst-looks and polished hair stares brightly at me. Here enveloped, annotated and filed is the process of maturity, frightening in its transience, its brevity, its gathering speed.

May 5.
Equity holds its annual meeting at the Apollo Theatre housing the comedy *Boeing-Boeing*. 'As good a giggle as to be had anywhere in London,' proclaims a poster outside. Hear a brilliant speech from a South African actor-producer, Cecil Williams, who was under house arrest for his anti-apartheid views. He makes a plea as impassioned as

42

any made by his leading men to Equity to stop members performing in South Africa. But the union decides to press its policy of trying to persuade the SA government to allow members to perform before multi-racial audiences.

A lot of time is taken up by debate on amateurs taking professionals' jobs. The names of Caroline Maudling, the Chancellor of the Exchequer's daughter, and boxer Terry Downs feature prominently. It is faintly incongruous to see familiar faces normally engaged on television loving, fighting and doctoring engrossed in resolutions, references back, referendums. It is also gratifying to see union business conducted with intelligence and common sense. The faces on the platform have the composure of success: Michael Denison, lawyer, Marius Goring, sadistic German officer, Robert Flemyng, schoolmaster, Richard Attenborough, Guinea Pig schoolboy, Maurice Kauffmann, who supplies the only theatrical touch with a pair of smoked glasses.

May 7.
Tenants of Church Commissioners' property in Little Venice, near Lord's cricket ground, have complained about the attitude of the agent for the property, Col. Hanbury-Bateman. Tenants who include Lord Norwich, novelist Elizabeth Jane Howard and James Ogilvy, stockbroker brother of the Royal bridegroom, allege that he has been rude. I meet the colonel and he is civility personified. He even poses for the photographer with a bowler sliding low over his forehead. I arrive home at eleven. The phone rings and I am told to catch a plane next morning to Nigeria where the government is trying to extradite Chief Enahoro from Britain to face treason charges.

May 9.
Lagos. I file a situationer about a country waiting for the return of an errant defendant. The trial of 21 other Africans charged with treason is in its 98th day. The judge has said that if defence counsel — there were 70 of them when the trial started — do not finish their speeches by the weekend

he will adjourn because he is exhausted. I meet Graham Lovell of Reuters and Denis Neeld of AP. They take me to an open-air nightclub for a drink. We drink beer in the warm moonlight and watch black couples shuffling and jerking to the High Life. Many of the girls are coquettishly pretty with straightened hair or wigs, tight jeans and chocolate skins. They dance with natural rhythm, making two white couples look as if they are dancing in splints. A fight breaks out in one corner. A large Nigerian aims a blow at a small Nigerian and misses. He is rewarded with swinging slap from girl. Most arguments in this part of the world are about land or women; his was presumably women.

The three of us drive to the beach at 1am and bathe in surf flung onto the shore by huge curling rollers. Crabs flee before us, frogs croak, the sea roars and spumes, advances and retreats, boils with anger. The leaning palms are tranquil in the moonlight.

May 10.
Invited to Dennis Neeld's flat for dinner. We watch television − *Perry Mason* followed by a disjointed news-reel − and gradually become aware of a steady dripping. Outside lightning as neon-blue as the television lights the sky, thunder cracks and rain bounces high in the black streets. We investigate and find a gutter is blocked and the balcony is a six-inch-deep paddling pool. We try to bale it out but our worthy efforts deteriorate into a water fight and we are all soaked. Water floods the bedroom and pours through the ceiling into the dining room beneath.

An African servant who had polished the furniture that morning gazes at the scene and says: 'Oh my lord, someone has been very silly here. Very silly indeed.' He eventually finds a peanut tin stuck in the gutter and the water disappears. We sit at the dripping dining table, soaked but exuberant, and drink whisky.

May 12.
Lagos lazes in the Sunday sun. Outside huts and houses

children wrestle in the dust; budding girls twist their hair into spikes; beautiful babies with velvet bodies recline trustfully on their mothers' backs. In the Ebenezer Baptist Church religion is making a lot of noise; predatory taxis swoop on pedestrians; boys selling cold drinks pedal white tricycles. The air-conditioned bar of the Bristol Hotel is cold and dead, white expatriates sip cold drinks and remember cricket and suburban gardens blooming with roses and mothballed courtships and Christmas snow. Hibiscus, flamboyant and bougainvillaea, lush with humidity, flower gaudily here, but none so creamily extravagant as almond blossom in a Harrow road. I watch fishermen catching mullet in white nets that parachute to the river-bed to snare the fish's gills. The mullet flap spasmodically, suck in the poisonous air and die shivering.

May 14.
A sticky day checking with lawyers, sending service cables, challenging taxi drivers, ignoring vendors of broken sun glasses and castrated ball-point pens. I read the newspapers − race riots in Alabama, political riots in Kenya, and in London. Here I marvel at the calm before the storm. People shop and dine and feed their pets with unaffected nonchalance that questions the inevitable violence. It was the same in the Congo, Cyprus, Algeria. I can stomach it all until children and old people get hurt. I can digest and excrete a mass slaughter but choke over the bewildered, bloodied face of one child.

May 16.
An early start at the airport to meet Enahoro, who was deported from Britain at 1am after a Commons slanging match. After waiting all day in sticky heat a DC-6 touches down and taxis to the end of the runway. The airport is surrounded by 100 or so riot police in jungle boots armed with truncheons, rifles, tear-gas bombs and wicker-work shields. The aircraft waits at the end of the runway and I notice a white van drive up to it. I suspect that Enahoro has

been taken off surreptitiously to avoid trouble. The DC-6 trundles up to the airport building and disgorges baggage, bodyguards and air hostesses. No Chief Enahoro. My suspicions are confirmed.

I drive into Lagos and confirm that he has arrived. He is in Ikoyi police station with truck-loads of police standing by. I find his lawyer in a nearby hotel and hear that Enahoro — surprise, surprise — is 'in good heart'. Scots photographer Harry Benson arrives on a scheduled flight with John Bulloch of the *Daily Telegraph*.

May 17.
Enahoro in court. Police, drunk with the success of yesterday's ruse, allow us to the rear entrance of the courthouse to see him arrive. The courtroom is a replica of an English court. Deep chuckles roll round the courtroom at the legal witticisms involved in Enahoro's appeal for bail.

Enahoro — a happy moustached extrovert — refuses to plead until his lawyer, Dingle Foot, Q.C., has seen the charges. I later learn that the Nigerian Government will not allow Foot to represent him. A bail plea is adjourned until Monday. Outside, Harry, lithe and efficient, hops around in the sun taking pictures of Enahoro, his wife and their chocolate-chubby daughter, Annabella. Harry radios pictures, I file a story, we fall into bed and drift into air-conditioned dreams.

May 19.
Saturday, nothing moving. Masochistically I go to the beach to take another beating from the breakers. A beach photographer offers to take a picture — me, Harry, John Bulloch, Dennis Neeld and Graham Lovell. We pose with folded arms like a five-man football team hoping to terrorise the opposition. The black cameraman has a big box on stilts. To expose the film he removes the screw-top from a coffee jar and counts three. When can we collect the prints? we ask. 'In five minutes, master.' He pours fluid into a drawer in the side of the box, plunges his hands through the aperture

46

draped with what looks like a black bedsock. And out comes a negative. He rushes this to the sea and washes it in a breaker. He then prints the negative, fumbling inside the bedsock, and within five minutes flat produces a perfectly good photograph. He duplicates five prints and charges 7s.6d.

I also meet Jack Solomons, boxing promoter, in Nigeria to make final arrangements for the Dick Tiger—Gene Fulmer middle-weight title fight. He wears a light brown suit, pink shirt, white silk tie. He asserts that on the night of the fight he will wear a gold agbada. He tries on one for us and emerges through the hole in the top like a badger contemplating the sun after long hibernation.

It is faintly incongruous to be interviewing him in this air-conditioned castle in the tropics instead of an office in petrol-fumed Great Windmill Street. He talks with affluent confidence and enthusiasm about boxers he has matched. They were all good boys, nice boys. Possibly the best, he reckons, was Randolph Turpin. He stays one day as if he were at Brighton and flies back in an aura of cigar smoke, after-shave lotion and knock-out reminiscences.

May 20.
Enahoro is in court again. He is refused bail. He wears a mustard-yellow agbada and looks more like Alfred Hinds every day. Later Harry Benson and I see Mrs Enahoro who runs a beauty salon in the suburbs of Lagos. Mostly she straightens hair and offers to straighten mine. She is a graceful woman with beautiful negroid features. They have three children — two in England, Annabella in Nigeria. She accepts the situation with serene stoicism that does not contradict her worry. I chat to her and Harry takes pictures while she straightens the hair of a pregnant woman who looks as though she may have quads.

We take the story and pictures to the airport to airfreight to London. The taxi costs £3 and the freight charge is £3.10s.7d. Back to the hotel for a beer at 4s.3d. a bottle. It must be one of the most expensive countries in the world; perhaps Jack Solomons was not so out of place.

47

May 23.

Dingle Foot, Q.C., has been banned from entering Nigeria and his junior, Kenneth Potter, flies in. He is pale and damp after the flight; he wears formal grey and looks a bit like Tony Hancock. He books into a small dark hotel with a big bare lounge that only Graham Greene or Somerset Maugham could animate. He is amiable, unnecessarily cagey and patently thoroughly enjoying the whole business.

May 25.

Harry, John Bulloch and myself watch a soccer match, Vasco da Gama versus Nigeria's Green Eagles. The ground is hard and balding and the grass has gone to seed. Dark faces lit by African smiles are wedged around the ground in banks and tiers of sporting fervour. Bright golfing umbrellas twirl in the sunlight; boys hang from the casuarina trees like ripe fruit; women squat splay-legged in grand robes printed Reckitt's blue from a local dye; two explosions in one corner of the pitch cause alarm but they prove to be an advertising stunt for a mineral water.

The Green Eagles start off in great form but their glory is brief. The Brazilians have internationals playing for them and they are soon toying with the labouring Nigerians, darting into wide open spaces, dribbling prettily, dummying, chipping, always plotting. They win 6−0.

May 26.

The British High Commission information officer, John Hall, invites us to the commission beach hut for a picnic lunch. He is tall, soft-spoken, sporting a fragment of greying beard. He was once in the news himself when he managed to get his Russian wife out of Moscow after a seven-year battle. They have five children − all their names begin with J − and they live in a gracious house with a garden filled with hibiscus, flamboyant, mangò, casuarina.

We wait for a launch to take us across the lagoon to the High Commissioner's luxurious coffee-bar style house. The

Commissioner, who is away at the moment, is Lord Head; he was War Minister at the time of Suez. The garden is an oasis with a tiny swimming pool, tennis court, Crown birds strutting the lawns and a Malayan baboon with a bright black face showing off in a cage.

We take the launch across the lagoon to the beach. I drink a beer, feed peanuts to the lizards and run across dunes embroidered with mauve couch grass to the breakers. I attempt to surf but am put to shame by small boys and fat women. Later I swim on another beach where the sea is as calm and warm as bath water. Bruised clouds gather, but a wise old expatriate reassures me: 'It will pass over – you can always tell.' Seconds later thunder rolls, lightning flashes and rain buckets down. 'It won't be much,' asserts the old hand. We crowd into a hut and eat sandwiches and mangoes and drink beer and smell the clean smell of rain on sand.

May 27.
I drive to Ibadan to cover a row between two politicians feuding over the premiership of the West Region. The Privy Council in London has ruled in favour of one of them; this has absolutely no effect on the local government which passes a resolution rejecting the Council's judgement. There is much excitement and 38 Action Group – Enahoro's faction – march out. Riot police ring the Assembly House, the gates are locked with handcuffs. A year ago members started fighting and police lobbed tear gas bombs inside. Ibadan is a shimmering huddle of tin-roofed shacks and houses converging on the new government buildings. Looking at its fetid poverty – burned-out lepers, beggars, balloon-bellied children – one cannot help pondering on the benefits the British are supposed to have brought to such countries as this.

June 1.
A week of humid endeavour draws to a close. I take the afternoon off to go to the races. The enclosure smells of watered grass and horses; the track is ankle-deep in sandy

soil. Each race has more than one odds-on runner and there is no place betting. No one, least of all the tiny black jockeys, seem surprised or excited by the results; this is not surprising as it is rare for the tote to pay more than 2−1. I back one winner but there is an instant objection which is sustained. None of the tension of a British race meeting is present; it is like having a quaint day out at Dymchurch instead of Brighton.

June 5.
I spend all day chasing a story about a team of Germans sent here to help form a Nigerian air force. I meet a Luftwaffe pilot who flew reconnaissance missions over Britain during the last war. He is small and tanned with chips of eyes that mirror blue skies. He was once chased back to France by Spitfires; when he was near the coast he went into a dive and pretended one engine had failed; the Spitfires let him go.

In the evening I hear on the radio that the Minister of War, John Profumo, has resigned, admitting that he lied when in the House of Commons last March, he denied impropriety with Christine Keeler. The Press has known most of the true facts for a long time but has been inhibited by Profumo's warning in March that he would issue writs for libel and slander if 'scandalous allegations' were repeated outside the Commons. The misfortune of Profumo was that he appears to have shared Miss Keeler's favours with Eugene Ivanov, second naval attaché at the Russian Embassy in London and presumably a spy. According to the radio, Profumo, in his letter to Macmillan, admitted that his deception was 'a gross misdemeanour'. You can't help feeling sorry for the man, stripped of his political future, stripped of his dignity, by a little indiscreet philandering. On the other hand he was a Minister of the Crown and he was guilty of the unforgivable: he was caught. I suppose this could bring down the Government. I also feel sorry for Macmillan, the only true British statesman to emerge since Churchill.

June 6.
A barber arrives at the hotel and we go to my room for my
hair to be sheared. He is grey-haired beneath an old green
cap. He snips away chattering about Australian football
teams, asking if I can tell him what teams to mark on his
pools. He interrupts his discourse to prophesy that I will be
bald within ten years. I tip him a shilling instead of two.

June 9.
Harry and I are winning the battle with the taxi drivers.
Once they tried to charge extortionately and claimed their
meters were not working. When we took the precaution of
asking if their meters were working they said yes – then
announced that the cable had broken during the ride. The
first break-through came when a driver claimed that the
meter had broken down and asked for 7s. The fare on the
meter was 1s.9d. and that was what we paid him. He looked
stupefied. There were more victories and word has spread
that we are hard men. The result is that now we always pay
according to the meter but have difficulty in getting a cab!
    There is, however, no sign of a break-through in tele-
phonic communication with room service. 'This is room
527 – tea and cakes for two please.' 'Room 408?' 'No,
527 – five two seven, five hundred and twenty-seven.' 'Four
two seven?' 'No, 527.' 'Ah, 527.' 'Yes, tea and cakes for
two, please.' 'For one?' 'No for 2 – two people.' 'You want
tea cakes?' 'Any kind of cakes – and tea for two.' Twenty
minutes later up comes a poached egg.

June 11.
Lightning laces the sky in television blue, thunder explodes
viciously and the night is awash with rain. Such a night Harry
and I pick to fly to Kano to write and photograph a feature
on a flying doctor service in Northern Nigeria. We slosh
from the car to the departure building and arrive as if we had
stepped out of the sea. In the plane I sit next to an engineer
who talks knowingly about African mentality. 'I sent my boy
out for toothpaste and he came back with toothbrushes,' he

says. 'He had forgotten what I asked for but preferred to apologise rather than query what I had said.' We book into the Central Hotel, Kano, rather like a holiday camp or a modern army camp with rank upon rank of clinical billets.

June 12.
We hire a car to take us to Gusau, which boasts the flying doctor. Ten miles out of Lagos the driver remembers that he has forgotten the spare wheel and we have to go back to get it. Twenty miles later we get a puncture and the spare wheel is substituted. On through the thinning bush, past skeletal trees, apple-green bushes, hillocks of elephant-grey rock like chunks of plasticine. We find the flying doctor and his team in three houses at the railhead town of Gusau, a gaggle of khaki, mud huts that smell of spice and sewage. There are three members of the team — a radio engineer, a former test pilot and Dr. Neil Duncan from Birmingham. The prefabricated houses were assembled by Youth Council members from Solihull, Birmingham.

We walk straight into a small tragedy. Four hours after the team's little red and cream aircraft touched down — after seven years of planning — a storm picked it up and broke its back. It is a write-off. God works in strange ways. This means that the succour that the interlopers planned to bring to villages plagued with cerebral meningitis, malaria and polio will be delayed while an insurance company debates the Act of God.

The doctor is an enthusiastic man with thin, tanned limbs, his altruism is fired by a love of Africa, a sense of belonging to the continent. The pilot, Tom Lampitt, is 31; he has a flier's flinty eyes and a young face; he is very proper and has a magnified sense of duty. The radio engineer, Fred Hunt, is a gusty, friendly Devonian formerly in the Nigerian police. The wives of Lampitt and Hunt deny that they are home-sick but their attitudes give them away — the eagerness to discuss home towns, inquiries about the weather and memories of soft summer days.

We leave them all in their bright blue homes with their

broken aeroplane waiting for far-off financiers to allow them to carry out their errands of mercy. We persuade our driver to get the spare wheel mended: a roadside mechanic with an air pump like a motor-mower melts a rubber patch on to the inner tube beneath an oil fire. The job takes an hour, costs 5s.

Later we have another puncture and on goes the mended spare tyre. We also run out of petrol because the driver did not like to disturb us while we were asleep. We stop at a village and pay the headman £1 — he gives us three gallons.

On through the murmuring night with eyes watching us from the bush; bats wheel, charge our headlights and soar away into the darkness; moths and bugs zip into the windscreen and die a milky blur. Seven hours after leaving the doctor we are back in Kano.

June 13.
We take a taxi tour round Kano. See craftsmen dyeing cloth in concrete vats of indigo sunk into the ground. Wherever you go in Nigeria women wear robes and head-dresses bathed in this bluest of blues. I peer into a hut where a man is beating the cloth so that it assumes a boot-polish brightness; it is a head-dress for an emir.

We wander through alleys flanked by mud walls containing huts and slumbering men. Stark-ribbed dogs snuffle in garbage, children with luminous eyes beg — 'Give us dash, master, give us penny, master' — old men stir and scratch in their baked dreams. The sky is broad, high and blue and there is no escape from the sun. This brown, glazed land is as unlike the south of Nigeria as the Yorkshire Moors are unlike the South Downs.

June 14.
Home again to Lagos. The familiar humidity, the conniving taxi drivers who have become undisciplined during our absence, the awaiting letters, the smiling receptionists — 'Hallow, Mister Lambaart — where the dickens have you been?'

53

June 18.

Our cat is well and her kittens have opened their eyes — slate-grey blinking slits. Harry and I found her prowling the hotel terrace, scared, thin and sagging-bellied. We followed her to her nest in a hedge and saw her newly-born kittens floundering and snouting in a heap of blindness. We feed her every day with milk and the fear has left her yellow eyes. I don't know where she goes when it rains but she is never wet.

Last night rain raced in from the sea and the hotel was cocooned in its noise. The terrace was deserted, marble floor spreading with puddles; outside the trees bowed and the fountain's jet of water collapsed and joined the rain; thunder cracked and the night was veined with lightning and a ship anchored in the lagoon was from another dimension.

Today it's placid and the sunlight is warm and mellow. The lagoon is like a pool of mercury. I buy pineapple and drink a contemplative lime juice while back in London the Profumo affair that has become the biggest political scandal of the century continues to reverberate.

June 25.

The Enahoro trial starts at last in a humid court room not unlike Bow Street. The prosecution case is not inspiring as far as copy is concerned (play cable next day says it made eight inches on page thirteen). Alun Davies, Q.C., displaces a manifest honesty, unmarred by ingenuousness. Astute, Welsh, likeable unless you happen to be under cross-examination. We sit from 9am until 1.30pm. I file too heavily but find myself unable to cut. I wouldn't make a sub.

July 1.

I get my recall. I shall miss the lagoon, ships becalmed on its molten silver, and the mauve sunsets. The thick air cloyed with jasmine — and less wholesome odours. The shuffling arrogance of black women in blue head-dresses. Waves on the beach climbing on each other's backs, falling in green

54

and white walls of spray. Begging children with beautifully curious eyes and swollen stomachs. Starlit nightclubs pulsing with High Life. The impossible phone calls, the rows with taxi drivers, the endless misunderstandings in which hilarity and frustration mingle. The asinine assumption of some Europeans, their misguided attempts to UNDERSTAND the common sense of those who have discovered humility.

July 2.
In Lagos at dawn but by late afternoon I am in South London playing cricket with the boys in a dusty green park smouldering with herbaceous fires of geums and poppies, its benches occupied by old men and women remembering. We row a bucket of a boat through the mossy waters of a pond. I admire the indifference of the people to our presence, their unconscious individuality, the creased clothes and soaped faces, the island sturdiness.

July 4.
Off to the Cotswolds for a few days' holiday. We stop for a beer at Hurley at a self-consciously antique pub containing comfortable chairs and angular customers. Beside us a family is about to reach a momentous decision: smoked salmon or caviar for first course. Salmon prevails. Thank God the tension has subsided. But also another crisis approaches when one of the youths decides on steak and spinach. He sinks back in his chair but is nudged by his sister, grey-costumed and sharp-nosed. 'What sort of spinach — fresh or purée?' The youth says he doesn't mind; not good enough. 'Fresh or purée?' 'Purée,' says the youth and the ghost of Popeye applauds.

On through B roads covered with spitting gravel, past fields and woods and heaths of blessed greenness. Abingdon, Lechlade, Cirencester, Stroud. We book into an old guest house with creaking stairs and beds. In the evening we drive through rain-washed sunlight to Laurie Lee's Slad. We see the T-shaped cottage where he lived in fine confusion with his mother and Doth and Marjorie and stand where the rainwater came tumbling down the hillside to swamp the kitchen.

'He often comes in for a drink,' says the landlady of the Woolpack. 'A quiet man always pulling on his pipe. Gets the bus every morning into Stroud to his office. Not like Jack. A film director now. There's a sharp one for you.' In fact Laurie Lee always said Jack was a sharp one back in those poor proud days when internal combustion was driving horses from the roads. But has so much changed here, vales and dales away from progress? The cottages are still stone, the voices as rounded as apples; sheep still graze and scabious still blossoms like tiny pin-cushions beneath sun-shades of elderberry blossom. There are cars and television masts and mechanical milkers and the seaside is nearer. But I doubt if the essence of Slad and the Slads all over the Cotswolds has changed. Laurie Lee corked it in a cider flagon.

July 5.
We drive to Cheltenham. When I was in the RAF it was a gracious city of queenly terraces, broad streets, wallflowers, a pub called the Plough, a hotel with disdainful pillars and a YMCA. This hasn't changed either. We dodge the soft rain, sheltering in bookshops where peaceful, powdery girls serve young men with umbrellas. A beer and on to Winchcombe. Hills rise and fall like waves in the summer rain.

We stop to eat sandwiches and listen to the commentary on the third Test match against the West Indians. We pass Broadway's curio shops and smart old hotels, and motor on to Stow-on-the-Wold — 'where the wind blows cold'. It is built around a square, bare and mellow and self-contained.

We book into an old hotel, clean and red-carpeted with an incongruous television in a bookish lounge. Our room overlooks a graveyard where the cropped grass has the special greenness that comes from bodies.

July 20.
A week-end in Brighton. Book into a seafront hotel with a

56

lift the size of a packing case, a dining room where old ladies in floral silk munch gummily behind vases of gypsophila and carnations and a small bar where dapper boozers tell racy jokes.

There is a small but unmistakable Brighton set. The men wear blazers and suede shoes, run second-hand Jaguars, make lunchtime bets over the evening papers; they seem prosperous but their source of income is not readily revealed. The women have bright cheeks and lacquered hair, tight two-piece suits, fur wraps, cunning corsets, empty gin glasses and a creaking propensity for flirting.

Off to the beach beside lounging boats, energetic dogs, apathetic waves.

July 21.
The sky is hazed with heat and the sea meets it in blue mist. A tranquil prelude to a brassy Brighton Sunday. Across the road to the shingle, off with our clothes. Men in vests roll up their trousers, freckled girls oil their bodies, panting women draw up skirts over dimpled thighs, youths with slender muscles gaze craftily at the girls who gaze out to sea. The great Sunday roast is about to begin.

Patrick and Martin squeal in the shallows, I paddle icily and watch my feet pale. Colonel Blimp, moustache dewed with sea water, floats cleverly with hands clutching his feet; a young man floats out to sea on an inflated mattress; a group of French boys and girls slap-and-tickle each other. The shingle shifts; ice-cream melts on clean skirts and trousers. We are eventually cut off by the tide and Elizabeth, with the aid of an aged gallant − not me − has to climb the sea wall.

No other town combines glorious belching vulgarity with faded elegance as effectively as Brighton. Regency terraces gaze with monocled eyes across green squares crowded with Cockney kids and girls in kiss-me-quick hats; the elegant Lanes lined with antique shops lead to the domains of postcards, warm beer, hungry slot-machines and coach parties who have light-aled their way down from London.

The two piers are antiques themselves. I hear a band

57

playing marches and waltzes, see mutton-chop whiskers and bonneted girls with trailing skirts, and mashers, now making old bones, seeing what the butler saw. Here are the same waves, the same anglers catching seaweed and crabs and eating sardine sandwiches on the rusty platforms.

'Can we have some pennies?' plead the children and they dive among the fruit machines and ancient football matches while we drink Guinness at the end of the pier and listen to three beefy Cockneys in straw hats flirting gustily with three beefy Cockney girls.

Back on the front and there, glory be, *is* a military band followed by marching soldiers. I lift Martin above the heads while the band plays his favourite song, 'Z Cars'. The driver of a police car looks embarrassed. Finally we leave the salty gaiety, vinegary winkles, flaking stucco of bygone dignity, piers with their domes like silver onions and head for home.

July 30.
The phone rings. Dr. Stephen Ward, osteopath, artist and student of Debrett's, who has been convicted at the Old Bailey of living off immoral earnings, has taken an overdose of drugs. I drive to the Chelsea flat where Ward, who was present when Profumo met Christine Keeler, has been staying. We all assume that the suicide attempt is not serious; how wrong we are. Photographers who arrived early to take routine pictures of Ward leaving for court on the last morning of his trial take photographs of him on a stretcher.

He is taken to St. Stephen's Hospital in the Fulham Road and the vigil begins. Reporters, photographers and girls in dark glasses gather outside. I don't think that Ward should have been tried let alone convicted. All he did was introduce girls to the titled and influential in a pathetic endeavour to be accepted in those circles. Now that a Minister of the Crown, John Profumo, has been forced to make a statement in the House about one of his girls, Christine Keeler, now that other *names* have been whispered, he has been dropped hastily by those with whom he sought to ingratiate himself and made a scapegoat for their philandering.

July 31.

Throughout the day Ward's condition deteriorates. I stay for 14 hours by the hospital which looks like a prison from the outside. Three times a day we have a Press conference with Mr William Mayne Butcher, hospital management secretary. Hospital-Press relations have improved a lot since I first became a reporter. Butcher is gentlemanly, reserved, helpful but medically unknowledgeable.

Sympathy grows for Ward. Bystanders speak bitterly about the rich and the famous who could have come forward at his trial to help him. He was, they say, a pawn in High Society lust, a lonely aesthete who only wanted to help. Pity for an underdog is once again triumphing. His paintings, his negatively handsome face, his friendly personality are remembered.

August 2.

Ward's life is ebbing. Again a full day at the hospital. Complications when the manager of a drug company roars up in his car under police escort. We understand him to say that he has brought a rare drug that the hospital asked for. Hospital-Press relations take a beating when Butcher expresses anger at the evening paper reports that they had called for the drug. There had never been such a request, he says. Ward's heart condition is worsening.

August 3.

Ward has been convicted. But the judge will never pronounce sentence. Ward died today.

August 20.

Holidays and we are motoring in the West Country. In Saunton where, as a National Service airman stationed at Chivenor, I once went for moody walks. I watch my ghost slouching through the dunes kicking tufts of sand with boots that steadfastly refused to accept a shine. My uniform has faded to threadbare grey, my forage cap slides over an ear.

59

The ghost is obsessed with the futility of his lot and hatred of his sergeant. I had recently shot a patient in the sick quarters where I was a medical orderly; I fired an air rifle in a corridor and the slug turned freakishly round a corner and hit a man suffering with carbuncles in the thigh. I also nearly killed a Rugby-playing officer who arrived at sick quarters asking for a pick-me-up after being kicked in the testicles. I gave him sal volatile but failed to add water. He clawed at his throat and fell to the ground claiming I had tried to kill him. He lived, but promotion to corporal was cancelled on the grounds that I was 'totally unsuitable'. The ghost also broods on the dearth of girls, the uncertainty of his future career, the lack of money to buy a bus ticket back to camp and the level of cigarette supplies that has sunk to two Woodbine butts.

August 26.
One of the most exciting Test series in cricket history reached its climax. If England bowl out the West Indians for less than 253 they will have drawn the series. I queue with Patrick for more than an hour beside the Oval's green gasometers. We are wedged between excitable West Indians. Many try to jump the queue but we make sure they are extracted by police. We sit on the billiard-table grass as Statham prepares to bowl the first over. Trueman bowls one over but leaves, pigeon-toed, with a bruised foot. He never returns and the England attack is shattered.

Hunt and Rodriquez prod away and wear down bowling which in any case is innocuous stuff on the lifeless pitch. West Indians hysterically applaud every hit. The game rollicks into life with the appearance of Kanhai who happily punches the ball through the gaps in the field. He wallops one six and falls on the backside. Wallops next one into the hands of Bolus. The West Indians win the game by eight wickets. As one commentator said when asked who he thought would win series: 'It doesn't matter − cricket has won.' Crowds surge across ground after the last hit. A voice pleads over louspeaker: 'Play the game. This is cricket, keep off the pitch.' Emotional scenes as Worrell and Dexter come on the pavilion balcony. And a forlorn Trueman. We return home after a contented sunny day replete with souvenir papers, score cards, green and willowy memories.

September 3.
I report outside Holloway Prison at 7am in case the Home Secretary frees a young bride jailed for contempt of court. Pimps wait for their girls to walk free at 8am; grubby men in dark glasses, mostly, but the girls seem pleased to see them. The jail is built like a castle; all it needs is a drawbridge. In and out go wardresses, chunky women in dark blue who look incongruous in the Camden Road.

What makes a woman do a job like that? 'Well, someone's got to do it, haven't they?' 'Yes, but why you? Someone's got to clean the toilets but you don't volunteer for the job.' It is somehow more obscene to contemplate the women locked up in Holloway than it is to contemplate men in prison.

The day mooches past. Up come the evening papers, late editions with all the losers; the pub on the corner opens its thirsty doors, girls in tight skirts hobble home. 'Keep Britain White,' says a slogan on the wall of this hopeless place.

September 6.
Back home again − to Lagos! The taxi drivers grin at their old antagonists; mosquitoes sharpen their stings.

September 7.
The High Court verdict on Enahoro. Fans whirr, a neon light stutters, pens scratch, the judge recites for 2½ hours. Finally the sentence: 15 years. It is stiffer than most people expected and there will doubtless be great lamentation from politicians, opportunists, idealists and cranks in Britain who claim he should not have been extradited.

September 11.
Chief Awolowo and twenty other defendants appear in court

61

for verdicts in a treason trial that started ten months ago. There are massive displays of police force in Lagos to strangle riots at birth. Red helicopters buzz around directing operations. I see a man mending his bicycle beaten on the head with truncheons, another pulled from beneath a lorry where he was hiding and clouted. It seems to be unnecessary violence. Nevertheless the police are highly efficient and there is no trouble. Awolowo, 'apostle of peace', gets 10 years for his part in a conspiracy that could have brought misery and bloodshed to the country.

September 20.
I hop over forest and sea in a Dakota to Lomé, capital of Togo, and observe the sophistication of Africans educated by the French; the British system does not emerge favourably from the comparison. Here there is little servility and all males are Monsieur – no masters. The French Africans also speak better French than the Anglicized Africans speak English.

Lomé is a strange, sad place, autumnal despite the palms, the clotted bougainvillaea, the rolling breakers. The broad promenade is deserted, palm fronds rasp and rustle. It is lushly tropical but as abandoned as Eastbourne on a wet November day. Yet eight months ago violence flared and President Sylvanus Olympio was assassinated in an army coup. Today they say it was all a nasty mistake – Lomé is that sort of place.

There are about 70 British in Togo. The hotel is square and white like most new African hotels. It smells of *tabac*, it's very smart and it's as lonely as the sea front. It also has a lighthouse at the bottom of the garden. It is separated from the sea by a swimming pool where children, brown and lithe, swim like otters. They have grey eyes and grace and confidence that our class system denies to many of our children.

September 24.
Back in Lagos most of the day is spent in my room writing a

feature about Togo. Later I go to the beach to cool off. The sand is still warm and evening-shadowed, curling breakers and flying spume lit with late sunlight. Behind the beach a white-robed priest calls his flock to worship with a handbell: men and women kneel in the sand and pray towards the sea. A boy with one blank eye leads his blind father along the beach begging sunbathers: 'Dash me a penny, master.'

Girls with falsetto voices, piano teeth and lovely eyes balance trays of coconuts, dirty bananas and green oranges on their heads and kneel beside me enticing me to buy. A half-caste African with ginger hair chants: 'Ice-cold drink, master.'

I walk back to the hotel along the road beside the lagoon. The sand is white and mixed with fragments of bone and shell. A black and white butterfly dances beside me, the sky is stained mauve and steamers slide past sensuously, parting the quicksilver waters.

September 26.
On the edge of the lagoon I discover an African fishing with a bell-shaped net that brings up hordes of small silver fish. But they are too small and he drops them on the hot concrete. They flap and pirouette on their tails pleading for water. Shamefacedly I pick one up and throw it into the water. The fisherman regards me warily. But the fish floats on the surface dead, already garbage: moments before it had been beautiful with life, a bright shekel from the lagoon bed. Lizards stare and curtsey. The fisherman picks his feet.

October 1.
Republic Day. A parade as British as the Changing of the Guard assembles on the racecourse. A band in starched white blows and thumps and awakes a medley of emotions — patriotism, love, pride. Soldiers in bottle-green, sailors and police slow-march past the saluting base. Dr. Nnamdi Azikiwe takes the salute. Then armoured cars with guns snouting, and a host of pretty children, playground drilled.

Outside, beer fizzes, mammies peel oranges, talking drums converse, a cavalcade of Africans dressed for no apparent reason as cowboys wanders through the crowds, stetsons bouncing on fuse-wire hair. An ocean of warm stout is drunk, big men dissolve into squeaking laughter. A glorious sweating bank holiday with the spectre of unemployment and poverty banished for 24 hours.

In the evening there is a reception in the grounds of State House. Huge women sit on tiny chairs. Girl Guides charge around with trays of drinks. Fairy lights and floodlights, the moon shining in black pools between the clouds.

The house, colonial and grand, has been here for 60 years or more. The Queen stayed here, Princess Alexandra presided cheerfully at an Independence reception. Now Zik is in residence. White diplomats flit among the gorgeous gowns swopping schoolboy humour with black politicians.

I meet the white inspector general of the police, a broad, sandy man. 'Twenty-eight years in the force, my dear chap. Loved every minute of it.' He complains about Press allegations of police brutality. 'Try writing about the good things of life, my dear chap,' is his advice for the night.

October 8.
Open day at Limehouse police station following an abrupt recall from Lagos. It is a debatable scheme to counteract the bad publicity the police have been receiving lately. Here stood Chinatown before it moved to Liverpool during the last war. Sax Rohmer's Dr. Fu Manchu indulged his opium fantasies in silken boudoirs behind peeling paintwork and creaking doors here; Thomas Burke stared into the river mist and wreathed tales about almond eyes that stared back; Jack the Ripper wet his lips and whet his knife in the shadows.

Into the police station pour housewives, children and one or two old customers. We are shown the charge room — bare and clean and hopeless containing a chair and a gauge on the wall for measuring clients' heights. The white-tiled cells look like bathless bathrooms. 'Centrally heated,' says our guide. 'The drunks like to come here. Get quite stroppy if they're taken to another nick.'

We see fingerprint equipment, a murder bag, a traffic meter, police horses and dogs and a Daimler Dart sports car for catching the ton-up boys.

The policemen are elaborately polite, not sure whether they approve of prospective customers wandering around their premises.

October 9.
Macmillan has been taken to hospital to have his prostate gland removed. Who will be his successor? Butler, Hailsham, Home or Maudling? I arrive at the hotel in Westminster where Rab Butler is staying at 6am. I go up to room 609 and see Mrs Butler. She is chatty, charming and still sleepy. 'Poor darling,' she says, 'he's having dreadful trouble with the telephone. But he's quite unruffled, you know.' Unruffled he certainly is − at 8.45am he is still in bed.

I catch the 12.25pm train with Butler to Manchester. From Manchester he is driving to Blackpool for the Tory Party Conference. He drinks a pink gin and eats a steak and kidney pie. He is courteous and uncommunicative. I enjoy being in a friendly Manchester pub for the first time in eight years. Once again everyone is 'luv'.

October 10.
I'm 34 today. I celebrate at the Old Bailey where a freelance journalist accused of indecency with Guardsmen alleges that an anonymous Tory minister is a homosexual!

October 12.
A golden Saturday lit with delicate sunshine; starlings gossiping, yellow leaves of lime trees flying like butterflies, fresh-spun gossamer floating on the amber air: girls with autumn eyes breast their way through the shopping crowds, boys crack conkers and knuckles, cats chase leaves, men wash cars.

I take Patrick to see Fulham play Nottingham Forest.

Blood-red shirts and white shirts on salad green. The players pant and sweat in this cricket weather and we agree that we could have played better ourselves. The game is a goalless draw but who cares on this day of rememberance — the burgeoning buds of spring, wet shingle, almond blossom, sixes hit over the lime trees; this day of anticipation — pillowed snow, nights iced with stars and Christmas candles.

'Buy yourself a pair of specs, ref . . . Kick him . . . knock him through the ground . . . dirty swine.' Girls hug their boyfriends' arms and pretend to enjoy the game because tonight there will be a visit to the cinema and visions of security and a kiss or two or maybe more in the back of a small polished car.

October 13.
Another session with Lord Hailsham, who has announced his intention to relinquish his peerage and be considered as a candidate for the premiership. Hailsham, Butler and Home, with Maudling dawdling behind, that's the line-up now. Hailsham appears outside his big, ramshackle house at 9.30am and we stroll to the edge of Wimbledon Common.

He is a charming, jovial man, a bit too volatile for his own good. He hurls himself into an emotion, a denunciation, a plea, and gets carried away by the rapids in which he may one day drown politically. Still, he is probably the most brilliant man in the party, gimmicks and all.

He denies that his poorhouse boots are a gimmick. 'I've got a bad ankle,' he explains. 'Boots are the best thing for it.' And adds: 'Don't have to darn your socks either.' And adds: 'Not that it matters these days with Terylene.'

We sit under a lime tree gently shedding its leaves. The grass is spangled with dew and there is a smell of damp leaves on the air. He is annoyed at jibes about his flamboyance. 'There is obviously support for me,' he says, 'and I have to take steps to make it possible for me to become prime minister.'

We later chat in his magnificently untidy study. He

66

expresses annoyance at statements in the Sunday papers that he had bathed at Blackpool. 'The water was freezing and the colour of chocolate éclairs,' he says. I look at some colour transparencies he took in Moscow and meet Lady Hailsham and some of his five children including the baby who is said to have lunched on Morecombe Bay shrimps. I am left with lasting impression of brilliant, boyish charm. He would have made a superb headmaster at Eton.

October 15 and 16.
Two days door-stepping the King Edward VII Hospital for Officers where Macmillan is recovering from his operation. One by one his henchmen parade at his bedside like schoolboys summoned to the headmaster's study. No successor for his job has yet been found. Hailsham bounces in, Home is courteous and enigmatic, Maudling as sombre as one of his speeches. All report that the Prime Minister is 'in good form'.

Rolls and Bentleys disgorge women in tweeds and limping men in regimental ties; there is something both touching and irritating about the reverence displayed by staff and visitors towards the star patient.

And still the Machiavellian struggle for power continues, as absorbing as a critical Test match or the first flight into space. The sunshine fades, rain drifts past discreet surgeries and waiting rooms, there is a smell of November and winter in the air. Photographers' flash-guns explode in blue belches, dusk thickens, the dynamo of power politics gathers momentum, the premier is still 'in good form'.

I have been keeping this diary for a year. As they say: 'It seems like only yesterday.'

October 18.
Macmillan resigns and Home gets the job. Macmillan was certainly one of our better premiers. He possessed a Thespian presence, a languid grit and a droll wit. I only recall him floundering once — during the Profumo affair.

67

His resignation was anticipated then but he survived majestically and it is only the surgeon's knife that has forced him to stand down.

October 21 and 22.
The Michaelmas daisy days dawdle past. I doorstep No.10 for the gathering of the reshuffled cabinet. Up sidle black Humbers with funereal drivers, out step the ministers waving chirpily to American tourists with Japanese cameras. Maudling wears a Reckitts-blue suit, Lord Home a vacant smile; Selwyn Lloyd is the chirpiest of them all, Soames charges in — bulkier than ever since he turned his attentions from war to agriculture; Butler is bland and thoughtful. I collect a 10s. parking meter fine.

October 30 and 31.
We get a tip that Roberta Cowell's father, Sir Ernest Cowell, is to remarry. His first wife died last year: his fiancée is in her mid-thirties. I confirm story but the couple are not to be found. Sir Ernest was Honorary Physician to King George VI.

Roberta, who underwent a sex-change operation in 1951, once stayed in my parents' ground-floor flat in Torquay. But my parents were blithely unaware of her identity. She left after a few months — perhaps when she learned that her landlord's son was a newspaperman.

I finally met her four years ago when she appeared for bankruptcy examination at Croydon. I still have a picture of her walking beside me in the high street. She was pleasant, unembarrassed by the stares of the curious and perfectly willing to discuss the change in her sex. She remembered my parents with fondness.

November 1.
A woman of 80 wins reasonable provision from her husband's will in the High Court. She had lived in comparative poverty for 43 years with an allowance varying from £3 to 30s. a week. She has brought up two daughters

and always believed her husband to be of moderate means. In fact he left £113,000, bequeathing £50,000 to Dr. Barnardo's Homes, nothing to her. She wins £1,000 a year for the rest of her life.

She tells me: 'I never dreamed he had all that money.' She lives with a daughter in Brixton amid towering furniture, old photographs and a piano. The rooms smell of lavender water and evoke the First World War. He was a sapper and married her in 1916. Then he went to Salonika. 'He was never the same after he had returned,' she tells me.

They lived in solid comfort on the outskirts of Nottingham, then parted. She sang at concerts, took in lodgers. The years mounted and she drew her allowance 'on condition that she remained chaste'. She tells me: 'He need never have worried about that — I was devoted to him.' Now she is white-haired, fragile and forgetful. And doesn't know what she will do with the money — except that she will be sensible. There is nothing to be done about the lost years.

November 3.
I drive to Brentwood to see the wife of do-it-yourself home decorator whose endeavours have forced them to sell their house. He has been at it for 12 years, hammering, painting, plastering, and has had two nervous breakdowns and a broken arm to prove it.

The house is old and gloomy in the darkening Sunday streets. The side door doesn't fit; two bare wires protrude from a hole where the door bell should be.

She is a jolly, trusting woman. They paid £1,300 for the house 12 years ago: now they are prepared to sell for £800. 'Anything to get a decent home for my three children,' she says. 'He's quite a good handyman, really, but things got on top of him. Once he climbed onto a tower of paint pots to replace a light bulb. The paint pots fell and he broke his arm.'

November 5.
A burglar steals jewellery and wedding gifts from Princess

Alexandra's house in Richmond Park. I spend the day in the park, rich and russet with sodden bracken. The Princess and Angus Ogilvy live in a fine Georgian house once owned by Sir Robert Walpole.

I speed home to let off the fireworks, sulphurous fires, witches' brews, fiery serpents, catherine wheels that don't wheel and rockets that remain firmly in the soil, hornets' nests, cosmic rays, fizzing bangers and jumping crackers that chase us round the garden.

The children are desperately excited as we take our place in the row of gardens already aflame with magnesium flares and Roman candles. Green and red stars melt in the sky, there is a distant chatter of gunfire. Then all is dead; there is no return: just the damp husks in the morning with lingering gunpowder odours and another 364 days to go until the garden is once again lit with cascades of emerald and brimstone fire.

November 6.
Up to the West End for lunch with my agent — a grandiose statement in view of my failure to publish a single book. We lunch at the Army and Navy Club. Half the people look like Osbert Lancaster. We hatch plans for my writing future over trout and white wine and Stilton.

November 9.
A birthday treat. I take Patrick to see Arsenal play West Ham. We roam around Highbury. It's an old, shabby, cut-price place, a Saturday shopping place, a London place. A small girl leads a man as old as Highbury by the sleeve; old men and women spend their pensions in the grocer's and corner pubs; babies suck their thumbs in prams outside pink-neon self-service stores and dimple happily as the wind comes up. Terraces with blistered paint and aproned women in the doorways point towards the shops. A wine store displaying dusty bottles with nothing tightly corked inside . . . a newsagent displaying dummy cigarettes, love story magazines and dead flies . . . prime cuts on parade at the

butcher's . . . stale pubs, second-hand junk shops . . . a poster advertising the game but someone has erased the *nal* from Arsenal.

November 10.
Remembrance Day in Whitehall. Poppies blooming on black lapels, medals jingling bravely. The Somme, Ypres, blood and mud and futility. Youths, puppy-keen and militarily spruce, prance and wheel to brassy bugle and hollow drum; old men preen their moustaches and tighten their puttees while shrivelled little women with pensioned faces try to remember the loss and feel only loneliness that has lasted for ever. And still arm-chair warriors try to make the memories glow: they died not in vain. But they did die in vain and there was no glory, only blood and mud and futility.

November 11.
A row has blown up in America about a Congressman who brought the head waiter from the House of Representatives' dining room on a NATO trip to Europe with him. I find the waiter, a grey-haired naturalized Jamaican, on the 21st floor of the London Hilton Hotel. He has a fluent rasping voice and is mightily sad about the furore his visit has caused. 'It has taken the beauty out of the trip,' he says. He thinks being a waiter in Britain is better than in the States – 'British people dine but Americans eat.' He says he has found no racial prejudice in Britain or France. 'In America if people don't like me for my colour I just don't have anything to do with them.' He is convinced that the row in Washington has been caused by the colour of his skin.

Later I interview Congressman Wayne Hays who brought the waiter with him. 'Next time,' he says, 'I'll bring a Red Indian.'

November 12.
An old man and his dog. The dog has been run over. At the pub where his owner collects glasses the regulars club

71

together and buy him another dog.

The pub is full of railwaymen in cloth caps who drink mild and bitter and eat pickled eggs. The old man drinks his beer enthusiastically as his new pet, a poodle, Duke, prances daintily at his feet. He is dressed in blue serge, wears his cap sideways and chuckles gummily as he recalls the habits of the poodle's predecessor, a mongrel. 'Used to dig up me taters, the bleeder.'

November 17.
Trafalgar Square for meeting of ex-jailbirds who want to form a trade union. Rain falls steadily and the pigeons who have recently witnessed some rum meetings in the square are sodden and plaintive. I talk to Mr Stanley Lowe who has spent 14 of his 40 years in prisons. He wears a velvet-collared coat, a Savile Row suit, carries an ebony cane and describes himself as The King of the Con Men − reformed. He tells the old lags gathered in the rain that he has done time in New York, Paris and Britain and is convinced that British jails are the worst in the world.

He tells me: 'I'm against the treatment that prisoners get when they come out. The law has had its pound of flesh. Why should men be victimized afterwards?' There is a splashing of applause and a few drowned cheers as speakers make their points, among them Lord Stonham, president of the Prison Reform Council. He claims that dogs and cats are better treated than discharged prisoners. Most speakers seem to forget that prison is intended as a punishment; nevertheless the system is bestial and should be reformed.

November 22.
A party given by the *Melbourne Herald* in their Fleet Street office. The first flash: President Kennedy shot at. Shock and disbelief. Another flash: wounded in head. The party disintegrates. I arrive back at the office to hear that last rites are being administered. Then − beyond even the compre-hension of journalists − he is dead.

The fallibility of mankind has been exposed. Great

concepts, great minds, great interpretations of civilization, are puny when a bullet fired by one crazy man can end the life of a great man.

The first edition goes straight on to the streets. White-uniformed sellers gather around Fleet Street exits, news-paper vans cause traffic jams. People stand transfixed reading the news. Our local, Poppins, is crushed with reporters and subs. The enormity of the tragedy is only now being felt after the tensions of getting the story into the paper. It is the biggest news story since the end of the last war, caused by a nonentity, a madman. Therein lies the enormity of it. The fallibility of us all.

November 23.
Craven Cottage, home of Fulham Football Club. Rattles are muted, cheers fade, scuffles unscuffle. A crowd of 22,000 stands silent and motionless in a cruel wind to honour the memory of President Kennedy. A throng with a fair ratio of rogues and hooligans stilled as if by a call from the unknown. A mob who have come to rave and cheer, to identify themselves with the players, to sweat out hatred of the boss and frustration with the wife, to relive their lusty youth, to join the game, to referee it, are transfixed by secondary shock.

Gone are the football league flags: in their place the Union Jack and the Stars and Stripes snap over river and pitch: the players, each wearing a black armband, face each other in sombre platoons. We hear a hymn, a child's cry is hushed, a rattle starts to cough and is stifled; programmes are held like prayer books. Then it is over. The crowd erupts. Time stopped has been restarted. Fulham beat Sheffield United 3−1.

November 24.
I watch the Duke of Edinburgh, Alec Douglas-Home and Wilson board a 707 to take them to Washington for the memorial service for Kennedy. Ring the office and hear that the man accused of assassinating Kennedy has himself been

shot. A small, stumpy man thrust a gun into his body. Again the mind reels. All Saturday we saw a small man with pouched eyes, receding hair and a twisted smile on TV; we presumed he was the killer; now he is dead.

December 5.
A man has been charged with uttering a threat to kill the Queen. I cover his committal for trial at the Mansion House. He is mentally disturbed and I cannot see the necessity for this legal rigmarole. Three jolly clergymen give evidence — he handed the threat to a priest taking Communion. He stares at his feet, a lonely figure in an open-necked shirt and straggly grey hair, unshaved because they took his razor away from him. He is committed and the sad business progresses a step further on its predestined, red-taped course.

December 6.
Lord Hailsham, now Mr Quintin Hogg, has been elected M.P. for Marylebone. A Young Liberal alleges that in the mêlée outside the Town Hall Mr Hogg punched him. Hogg denies this. I interview the Young Liberal in the Lobby of the House of Commons, observed by a flunkey in white tie. The Young Liberal is young and ardent and outraged. He was, he says, trying to hold up a Votes-at-18 poster in front of Hogg. This was snatched away and he was punched by Hogg. 'I was shocked,' he outrages. 'Wouldn't you be?'

He clutches a Stetson hat, sports an orange Young Liberal badge and enjoys it all mightily. The Young Liberals tell me proudly they were only jeering and sneering at Hogg. Whatever happened my sympathies lie with the big-booted, amiable politician.

December 21.
A sparkling day rimed with frost. Into the car and off to Chipstead Downs to gather holly and ivy. The grass on the slopes where I once tobogganed droops with frost, our breath smokes and Christmas excitement stirs.

I drink a pint of mild in the Mint and supply the children with cheese-and-onion-flavoured crisps which they dislike. At Rose Hill I buy a large Christmas tree for 10s., a magnificent conical conifer. We plant it in a bucket in the corner of the lounge and drape it with tinfoil icicles, tinsel frost, Chinese lanterns, glass baubles and bells as light as spun sugar.

December 22.
In the morning I roam round the Tower with photographer Terry Fincher looking for a man charged with threatening to murder his wife's lover who has been given bail provided he stays with his brother who is a caretaker here.

We march into the residential quarters with surprising ease and the brother comes to the door demanding: 'How did you get here?' We just walked in, we say. 'Blimey,' he says, 'wait till the governor hears about this.'

December 23.
5am. The phone shrills. Off to Gatwick Airport, they say. A liner, the *Lakonia*, on a sunshine cruise with 1,000 people on board, is on fire; passengers have taken to the boats. A hire car arrives; off we go through fog, two wire men and photographer Leslie Lee.

I don't think we'll make it — fog swirls thickly around us — but we do. I meet John Weaver at Gatwick. But no planes are taking off due to fog. Finally we take off at 10am in a chartered Viscount. Refuel at Lisbon and head into the Atlantic looking for the *Lakonia*. Sight her at 3.40pm. Rescue ships standing like mourners around the dying ship. Smoke rises and melds with the clouds, fires burn crisply from stem to stern. There is no sign of survivors. We circle five times while photographers take pictures. She leans heavily in the water like an invalid with a stick, smoke idling from her funnels, a blazing gravestone of a sunshine cruise.

We return to Lisbon and the usual frantic efforts to contact London. Laymen probably believe that the chief difficulty of reporting is getting the story. Wrong. The

75

nightmare is always getting rid of it; no point in having a story if you can't communicate it. We swallow a quick drink and sandwich and board a chartered Constellation for Madeira, where survivors will be landed. We arrive at midnight at Porto Santo and take the ferry to Funchal, capital of Madeira, 40 miles away.

December 24.
I contact our woman stringer who says she doubts if she can help us this morning because she has to do her Christmas shopping. Wait on the quay for arrival of mercy ships. Dawn breaks. Funchal is piled across the harbour, reddish houses inserted on terraces up steep hillsides. The lights go out, a snow-capped mountain emerges from the night. Ambulances range behind us, the sea laps plaintively.

The first rescue ship berths, the liner *Stratheden*. Three stretcher cases are taken off − two women, sad and disarrayed, not caring who sees them. Perhaps they had saved all their lives for this cruise. Then an old Greek seaman, waxenfaced, soles of his feet caked with salt. He looks bad. The *Stratheden* took on one young German seaman: he was incoherent when they took him aboard and he died later.

The next mercy vessel is an old passenger ship, the *Salta*. Men, women, children line the rails shouting to us. As they leave the ships in blankets, pyjamas and evening dress, many allege panic by the crew of the *Lakonia*, insufficient lifeboat drill, rescue equipment that didn't work. A woman, youngish with neat hair, tells me that she last saw her husband standing on the burning decks of the *Lakonia*. I observe her for three more days, watching the survivors' lists, slowly losing hope. He is never found.

The tragedy would be overwhelming if we were not immersed once more in writing and getting the copy out. Unfortunately there are no papers in England on Christmas or Boxing Day and we are writing only for the Scottish edition.

Christmas Day.

In the streets, intricately cobbled in whorls and loops, young men take orchids, yellow and brown and leopard-spotted, to their girls. Bougainvillaea blooms in lazy tresses, bird of paradise flowers peer beakily from vases in the hotels.

The survivors from the *Lakonia* crowd the cable office, wait beside the phones. A blonde girl in her teens reads a list of survivors and collapses weeping. The reactions of people in distress vary astonishingly. The shipping line gives them £10 each to buy clothes; some women haggle in the shops and debate the colours that suit them; most women are calm and heroic as they await news of husbands and sons, some men break down.

Greek sailors squabble and moodily drink Madeira wine. But the overall impression is one of quiet bravery blending with the companionship of distress.

December 26.

No ferries sailing because of storms charging the isle of sunshine. Torrential rain streams down the cobbled hills and lashes the banana trees. The island has lush beauty, no beaches. Behind the luxury of Reid's Hotel, the Savoy, the clubs, lurks terrible poverty. Many survivors have now left; the rest, apart from the bereaved, have regained their spirits and the businessmen with their mild, powdered wives plan claims for damages. Baggy-eyed and wearing a heavy-knit sweater, I am frequently mistaken for a survivor.

December 27.

We sail for Porto Santo on the ferry. An accountant, pale face discoloured by a black eye, tells me he was crushed between a lifeboat and the *Lakonia*. His wife, who saw it happen, brings him tea. The ship rolls in the swell and the accountant lies on the deck. He tells me they will have to operate on him when he gets home.

The man I have liked best so far is a London cabby, as Cockney as Cable Street. He stood in a lifeboat with water lapping his waist for 10 hours holding his baby boy Freddie.

Freddie's body grew stiff and cold and his father kissed his face to keep it warm. When he was taken on to the *Salta* they thought the boy was dead. But with the resilience of extreme youth he recovered. We left Freddie in a Madeira nursing home chuckling through the salt water burns on his face. Said his father: 'I know it's silly but I reckon God looked after that little boy of mine.'

December 28.
Take off for London. Back to crackers, presents, turkey scraps, Christmas pud. But I sleep fitfully, twitching, and waking with a start. I cannot yet forget the bereaved, mothers, fathers, husbands, wives. Stories of babies floating, dead; men sucked beneath propellers while their wives watched helplessly.

1964

January 11.
Hectic day finishing revisions to my precocious autobiography *The Sheltered Days*. Take MS to a typist, Mrs Roslyn Kloegman, on the way to the airport to catch a plane to Cyprus.

January 12.
Land at dawn in Nicosia, my third visit. I was first here in 1956 when Eoka terrorism was at its height. The scents of the island are familiar, spicy and smoky. I meet many old friends at the Ledra Palace Hotel: Savas, the night porter who can fix most things on the island, Stelios, the barman who never loses at dice, photographer Terry Fincher, Ronnie Robson from the BBC, Harry Miller from the *Telegraph* and many others.

Terry drives me around Nicosia and I see the homes in the Turkish quarter wrecked by the Greeks. British troops still occupy No-man's land between the two warring races. They look tough and sensible in this sustained atmosphere of hysteria but none of them seems to know if they should fire if fired at.

Across parched plains the Kyrenia mountains are mauve, curdled with clouds at their peaks. Terry shows me a photograph of a Turkish woman and her children, dead and bloodstained, in a bath, faces serene and unsuspecting. An adult atrocity in a children's world of trust.

January 13.

I drive to a village where the Turks are exhuming the bodies of twenty of their countrymen butchered during the Christmas massacre. The corpses are in an advanced state of decomposition, curled in grotesque attitudes.

The graveyard is ringed by British paratroopers and it is reassuring to hear Geordie, Scouse and cockney accents as the macabre business progresses.

A few hundred yards away Greeks gather to watch the exhumation. Nine of the bodies are believed to be Turks who live there – seven men, a woman and a child. The Greeks deny any knowledge of the atrocities. The Turks, they say, left the village 'on a journey'.

January 16.

A wild night at paratroop sergeants' mess. Hear flinty stories about their training course and meet tough RC padre who drinks his drink and sings his songs with the best of them. We carouse most of the night and take part in a sophisticated drinking contest – who can get the booze down their throats the quickest. We lose but understand the paras cheated.

January 17.

Into Durrell country with Harry Miller of the *Daily Telegraph*, who shares the same sense of humour as myself, with the result that we converse in explosions of laughter. Kyrenia, with its old walls and sun-dazed buildings, is deserted; hungry dogs prowl voraciously and lemons and oranges fall unplucked. From the mountains the sea is a dozen shades of blue, permed into white waves by an iced wind. Last night there was a white frost, the first many Cypriots have seen.

We lunch in the Hesperides, a white sea-front hotel designed for sunshine and peace. We are the only customers in the bar. The wind makes the fear in the streets outside tangible.

We drive into the Turkish quarter and see refugees arriving from villages where they are surrounded by Greeks. A brazier burns fiercely outside a shop; inside we talk to a Turk who was beaten up during the fighting. 'Makarios will be assassinated,' he says. 'Nicos Sampson is wounded,' he says. Wishful thinking.

We drive back through the mountains where the crusaders fought, past St. Hilarion Castle which Walt Disney is said to have used as a model for the castle in *Snow White and the Seven Dwarfs*, past harsh Wild West peaks, through Turk road blocks where nervous, muffled guards tell us not to drive so fast.

January 23.
I fly to Athens in a dazzling Comet following tip that the former Greek Cypriot guerilla leader, Grivas, has flown there to confer with more than 100 'freedom fighters'. I book into the King George Hotel, a splendid, silent pile. I walk round the grounds of Parliament House; citrus groves and ponds fat with goldfish. I observe two lovers holding hands beneath an orange tree, lost in each other's eyes.

Outside the streets bustle with homeward crowds. The girls are as groomed and graceful as the girls of Lisbon but more type-cast than the girls of London. Their hair is back-swept and they wear silk scarves and leather coats.

January 24.
I try without success to find Nicos Sampson, a leading henchman of Grivas and wander down broad streets to the old town. I adjourn to coffee shop for sandwiches and ouzo, the white anis of Greece. I like it but if I was told it was cough medicine I wouldn't disagree.

I visit the Acropolis and survey Athens spilled beneath. In the distance the crumpled mountains are veined with snow. A cold wind sighs through the pillars; American voices gee-whizz across the desolate grandeur of eternity. A bald guide with a large nose points out the monuments to me prefacing everything with 'Please, mister . . . '

81

I emerge from the past and take a taxi to the airport to meet Greek-Cypriots flying in to meet Grivas. Sunset lights the sky; fairy lights of the American naval presence light up prettily. In the middle of a lot of excited Greek-Cypriots stands a forlorn little man who looks like the actor Adolph Menjou: it is Grivas. He resembles an undertaker, a bank manager, a salesman in a gas showroom: he is a retired terrorist leader responsible for untold death and bloodshed who eluded the British for four years.

He declines to talk and sits rather sulkily beneath a customs sign. A charter plane trundles to a halt and out spill his old comrades; they kiss his hands, his cheeks. He wears a grey hat and long funereal coat. Off they go after posing for pictures — lawyers, mayors, politicians, retired gunmen. Grivas is driven away in a black Cadillac.

January 25.

I attend a meeting of the Chamber of Commerce convened for Grivas. After the recent Greek-Turkish fighting he must, he says, break his silence. Break it he does. He implies that he is going to enter Cypriot politics at a distance. The overthrow of Makarios is manifestly his objective. The gathering applauds frenetically: independence has been a bit of a wash-out and they are happy to be back with a vociferous grievance.

Later I take a taxi to the port of Piraeus. The driver, who doesn't speak English — just a lot of 'nays' which mean yes and wouldn't do him much good in Yorkshire — charges up unmade roads as steep as a mountainside. He keeps leaping out and gabbling to bystanders as we climb higher and higher. He is an old man and I don't like to shout at him. We plunge down an alarming descent apparently on our way to Turkey. I shout 'Over there', and he nods wisely and says 'Nay'. Finally we end up at our point of departure. I give him 80 drachmas and he says 'Nay'.

White boats are tethered around Piraeus harbour, sailors on the quay sway with the movement of the waves; the air smells of salt, ships, paint, coal smoke.

It is dark now; locust flocks of starlings envelop a church and the people of Piraeus swarm into the meat market. An old man walks past with a small girl, ragged and poor, young and old, a unit of poverty, a unit of trust.

I visit a grocer's full of crystallised fruits, honey sweetmeats, spices and plump girls. A flea-pit cinema advertises a sex film; teenagers gawp at the stills and chew nuts slowly. Kiosks sell nuts and copies of *English Beauties* who do not look in the least bit beautiful.

January 26.
Sunday morning, mellow and chiming, tranquil and trusting. I buy an ouzo on the boulevard of Constitution Square. The sunshine lights pearls in the milky liquid and the ice tinkles Sunday music. The square is big and broad, full of space, orange trees and photographers with ancient cameras. On one side stands Parliament House; other buildings are spiked with airline signs like TV masts. A boy whose shoes need cleaning comes and cleans mine with shoe polish like black oil. I light a cigar and the smoke smells good this Sunday morning; the cigar tastes bad. All the girls have the same hair-styles, sleek, springy and back-combed. The same eyes, too. Mothers and fathers, aunts and uncles and a grandma or two sit at tables drinking coffee and water. The sun flashes on a thousand pair of sun-glasses. It is time for lunch.

January 27.
The story is drawing to a close. Book myself on tomorrow's plane to London. Sunday siesta is over for a week; police with whistles harass pedestrians waiting to cross the roads, bright sunlight bouncing on their fireman's helmets. The sky is burnished blue and the Acropolis is a fragile iced cake in its glare. I know how tourists feel outside Buckingham Palace willing a roll of drums to herald past pageantry and seeing only a queue of taxis; penetrating the East End hoping the fog will roll back to reveal Jack the Ripper and seeing a bingo hall. I drink a last ouzo on a boulevard.

Pigeons puff and pout, ignoring a dirty grey cat which might once have been white.

What shall I take back from Cyprus? The blue of the sea at Kyrenia; the eerie sadness of Durrell's village where the friendliness he knew has been dissipated; the lemons and tangerines wasting beneath their parent trees; Cockney and Geordie accents as reassuring as a handshake; the puppy eagerness of Savas the Ledra Palace evening porter who has been Mr Fixit to the Press for ten years; the futile hatreds burgeoning from playground to death; the weals on the backs of the Greeks and the smell of decayed flesh as they dug up Turkish bodies still with combat boots on; drinking Turkish coffee in the Greek quarter; a belly dancer's belly in a deserted night club; the alarms, the rumours, so few knowing why they hate; guns firing at shadows. Senseless suffering.

And in Greece? The pearl-grey light in ouzo, puffed pigeons, parks mapped with orange and lemon groves, hard sunlight reflected from snow-salted mountains. Past and present closeted together. Girls with glowing skins and dark eyes, pastry smells, and food wrapped in olive leaves. Soldiers in skirts and stockings. Greek delight and Greek coffee.

February 2.
Visit Speakers' Corner to see a young man who decided to make his maiden speech there. He was half way through it when an old man called George punched him on the nose. I meet the aggrieved young man by the new fountains. He is eager and sixteen years old. His supporters wear Russian fur hats and dark glasses although it is a gloomy day. They are puppy keen and proud of the incident although their hero is reluctant to seek out George.

February 3.
Allegations in their university magazine that the Oxford boat race team has been drinking too much and generally living the soft life. Down to Henley-on-Thames to investigate.

Go into the Leander Boat Club and meet lugubrious man in soiled yachting trousers drinking beer at the bar. I discover after a facetious start, on my part, to the conversation that he is Jumbo Edwards, the Oxford coach. The rest of the crew arrive and are non-committal. Jumbo draws me aside. Now for the great revelation, the angry rebuttal. I listen closely as he mumbles: 'When you've finished your beer would you please leave − this is a private club.' He emerges later, bloodhound face pensive below a tiny yachting cap, and invites me to follow the crew in a launch. I do this for an hour and a half in lashing rain. Sky, fields and river meet beneath a grey veil; it is brooding and desolate on the river today. The eight strain, oars feathering the water, and Jumbo issues polite instruction through a megaphone. I watch water collecting in the folds of my sheepskin coat and spilling in rivulets down my trousers. Afterwards the crew, who do not look particularly muscular, perform back-breaking exercises and Jumbo mellows sufficiently to discuss their training. They are allowed 1½ pints of beer a day but no cigarettes. Build? 'About your physique,' he says looking at me speculatively. I squelch away for hot tea and toasted tea-cakes at a nearby olde worlde bun shop.

February 4.
Valentina Tereshkova, Russia's spacewoman, arrives in Britain. I meet her at London Airport. She is a robust girl, smart, lacquered hair, no make-up. She delivers good-humoured platitudes and says she would like to be the first woman on the moon. Much of this is a diplomatic recitation gulped down by TV. I speak to her later outside the Russian Embassy. Her comments suffer from interpretation. 'Women will never leave men alone in space.'

February 6.
Veteran bandleader Roy Fox wins his discharge from bankruptcy. He owes more than £9,000 and has paid off a total of £55 in 12 years. But apparently he is not legally obliged to repay any more. The advantage of bankruptcy to

creditors escapes me. I have a drink with Mr Fox who was at the top of his profession in the '30s — the era of big band shows. He played at the Kit-Kat and the Café de Paris. Among his singers was Al Bowlly, the idol of the end of that decade who was killed in the Blitz.

Fox is bald, elfin-faced, sober-suited, unrecognised. 'The hard winter of 1946 finished me,' he says. 'I came back from America and toured British music halls. But they were half empty because of the freeze-up.' How did Joe Loss — his relief band in the '30s — and others suvive? 'They went to the Palais,' says Fox. 'A thing I could never do.' The man whose signature tune 'Whispering' once enthralled millions finished his whisky and left the pub in Kingsway. Unrecognised.

February 8.
Drive Elizabeth and the children through fog into countryside lit with sleepy sunshine. See a bad crash on the way — a Mini and an old banger have collided and wrecked each other and a police car appears to have run into the back of the Mini. We have a drink in Rusper in a mellow old pub filled with dachshunds and their owners. Afterwards a muddy game of football in a recreation ground. We drive on to Crawley for lunch and get booked by a policeman who says I crossed a zebra crossing while a pedestrian was on it. I'm sure I did no such thing but I have a feeling that his word will be taken against mine at the magistrates' court. We inspect and dislike Crawley — new shopping parades, holiday camp image, absence of atmosphere.

February 11.
Middlesex Sessions in Parliament Square where Tottenham Hotspur winger Terry Dyson faces a charge of receiving stolen cigarettes. Police do not allow the Press to sit in the well of the court so we climb into the gallery where I am warned that if I peer over the rail to see what's going on I will be ejected. We protest during the lunch adjournment and we are allowed into the court 'provided you behave yourselves'. The case against Dyson, said to be the smallest

86

winger in first class football, is thrown out and rightly so — he apparently received the cigarettes from a fan and the operative phrase in the charge is 'knowing them to have been stolen'.

February 12.
The Rector of Spaxton, Somerset, is to give a service of curses — a commination service. I take the train to Bristol where Kingsley Squire, a member of our staff there, meets me and drives me to Spaxton. The church is small and cold, the rector large and benign. The congregation, Press apart, consists of seven women wearing woolly hats and one man. For years the rector has been involved in a feud with a section of the populace and has laid a curse on those who lay false information to the Bishop and the Press — an uneasy partnership. The commination service is in the prayer book and, according to the rector, has Biblical authority. The tenth curse, like a section of the Queen's regulations, embraces almost every sin — fornication, adultery, covetousness, extortion. The women intone the responses with enthusiasm.

I have a few drinks in the village pub and discover that the cows have not run dry and no one has turned into a frog. I stay in what used to be a good old hotel in Bristol but is now a miniature Hilton.

February 13.
I roam around the dignified streets of Bristol, past coffee shops and somnolent churches, through the fruit market with its orange smells. Back to London by train. The Cyprus situation seems to be blowing up again. More Turkish-Cypriots killed, Turkey poised to invade. I learn that Patrick has passed his eleven-plus; hear my autobiography about a childhood in the last war has been turned down by Hutchinsons even though they enthused about it.

March 20.
After several weeks of ennui I decide to resume the diary.

87

Catalyst: the Beatles. If you have any pretensions to being a diarist you surely cannot meet the Beatles and not record the meeting. I meet them at Television House; well, three of them − Ringo, Paul and John. And get their autographs for Patrick. They are cute, wise young men somewhat obsessed with the money they have made and the fact they'll never want. Who can blame them? Ringo is smaller than you expect, quiet and pensive; Paul is the voice of sanity; John is quick and clever and inclined to boast. I can only make a cursory attempt to explain Beatlemania: they are talented, wholesome and bright.

Outside small girls in old clothes shove a thick line of police; a couple dissolve into hysteria and are carried into the vestibule screaming and crying: 'I luv them.' A small boy in blue yells in bewilderment at the frenzy around him. The young lords leave under heavy police protection; half an hour later groups of girls are still roaming the rain-swept streets screaming and squealing.

April 10.
I am about to drive to Margate where teenage gangs have been fighting again when I am told to fly to Cyprus instead. So I will leave Elizabeth with all the problems of buying and selling a house but there is nothing I can do. She drives me to the airport in teeming rain.

The aircraft is a 707. Behind me sits a little old Greek-Cypriot wearing a deaf aid; because he cannot hear anyone properly he bellows in a cracked voice that he can speak five languages fluently. At Athens airport he waits for an hour until a hostess says we can reboard the plane, then goes to the toilet.

April 11.
We land at 6am. The sunshine is clean and warm and the island is green after rain. I meet my old sparring partner, Harry Benson, at the Ledra Palace Hotel and reporter Dennis Harper. Within an hour of landing I am scaling a peak in the Kyrenia mountains. The Turks are dug in facing

Greeks shooting from neighbouring peaks. After climbing for an hour and a half we are 2,400 feet up. The craggy slopes are scattered with boulders and thorn bushes and embroidered with red and white alpine flowers. We join the Turks, brown, moustached and wary, and peer across the prairie beneath. Guns fire in our direction and a Turk remarks placidly: 'We think they are going to mortar us.' Beautiful views of Kyrenia flattened below us beside the azure sea. I notice an old Turk on a donkey listening to a walkie-talkie radio. We descend through bushes and boulders and olive trees, watched by shepherds – a hazardous occupation these days – and their sheep. I am told that the mountains were once used to make a Wild West film: it needs more than Matt Dillon to stop this battle.

April 12.
I tour Nicosia seeing contacts – Canadians, British, Irish, Swedes, all in their United Nations blue berets. The Greek Cypriots openly laugh at their ineffectuality. I get caught in a street battle in Ledra Street, named Murder Mile in the '50s when the targets were the British. I flatten myself against a wall while villainous characters looking for trouble scuffle past, guns at the ready. Every time you pop your head round the corner bullets start flying. Earlier the Turks shot dead a middle-aged man pushing his barrow of haberdashery; an old woman putting out her washing was shot in the shoulder.

April 14.
I find a butterfly caught in the grille of a car. It is dying and I take it to be a swallowtail, almost extinct in Britain. I carry its fragile dead beauty back to the hotel. Call at a farm in the line of fire beneath the Kyrenia mountains and find the paras milking the cows. They had found the cows' udders distended with milk, the cows bellowing with pain. It is a bizarre scene, a model farmyard put together by a child – a ferret car, paratroopers feeding pigs, Wild West mountains in the background and a red British-style telephone kiosk in the foreground. I adjourn to an officer's house for lunchtime

drinks and meet, of all people, Harold Behrens who used to be in a crazy radio programme called *Where Ignorance is Bliss*. He is a small, sun-tanned Glaswegian not unlike Grivas. I also meet Judy Shirley who used to sing the introductory song to another old radio show, *Monday Night at Eight*.

April 15.
I drive to Bellapais, Durrell's village, and drink orange juice beside the Tree of Idleness. A Cornish village set in the Kyrenia mountains. Durrell's house, whitewashed and blue-shuttered, is still as he described it. And the bitter lemons are still growing in the garden.

April 19.
Drive to the village of Ayios Theodhoros where a battle is raging. As I arrive with Don Wise, the elegant pirate working for the *Mirror* who used to work for the *Express*, shots crack out and we cross a bridge dividing Turks from Greeks. The village is a dusty, dust-coloured assortment of hovels divided by a dried-up river bed where dogs sleep in the hot sun and a donkey has just given birth to a foal. A platoon of British troops in UNO berets of futile blue are based in a corner café; bullets sing past and crack into the wall of the café. 'Fuck 'em,' say the soldiers, brown and bad-toothed. 'Fuck the fuckers.'

An officer, young and decent, explains: 'There's a neurotic old bugger up the road who keeps letting off his shotgun. Every time we negotiate a ceasefire he blasts off again and the Turks fire back.' We christen the neurotic old bugger neurosides — and he promptly discharges his musket with thunderous petulance. We make friends with dogs who all look Dalmatian and faintly absurd, astounded at being stroked instead of kicked. I drink a beer in a little café as the battle continues to explode.

Later I tour both Turk and Greek quarters with an Inniskilling patrol. A small sturdy officer shouts at the unresponsive buildings: 'Stop shooting and the others will

90

stop shooting at you.' Finally he receives an answer – a volley of shots. But he marches on with 'fuck 'em all' valour. I am struck once more by the transformation that takes place in British soldiers when they arrive in situations like this: there is a sun-burned toughness, a cocky resilience about them that you would never suspect seeing them in an Aldershot pub. Officers, from the Paras, Foresters, Gunners, Skins, also seem to have acquired a new bearing.

The patrol returns and the shooting continues with sporadic futility. The sky is burning-blue and the hills are grey, pimpled with bushes. Where are the Sioux? Where is Maverick? I return to Nicosia with relief and vague surprise that I have not been shot. I am convinced that bravery is fatalism, particularly on this island, where they have lived with violent death for ten years. Shame is probably part of it, too. You can't make a fool of yourself in front of your mates.

April 20.
Return to the same wretched place. This time the bullets are being fired at *us*. We jump for it and make weak jokes to hide our fear. A Greek police inspector is helping with peace negotiations. He is a calm, tired man in his forties. Desk-bound for years, incongruous in his tin helmet. He never wanted war, this man, and he wears a collar and tie under his battle blouse to emphasize his stance. But he is willing to help his brethren by persuading them to stop shooting. I take a photograph of him drinking lemon squash with a British major and plan to bring the picture back when I return.

April 21.
No need to take the picture back. The inspector was shot in the heart after I left the village and died within twenty minutes. He told British soldiers: 'I know I'm going to die.' And apologized for being unable to keep a dinner appointment with a British officer. He died without complaint, this man who never wanted war.

April 26.
I take time off to go goggling in crystal waters around
Kyrenia. I gaze at a remote world, silent and moving with
the tide and forget the world above. Tiny transparent fish
dart and hover beneath me; bigger fish lurk in hollows in the
rocks and gaze at me, the intruder. The rocks grow higher,
chasms deepen, fields of seaweed move with the current as a
field of corn moves with the breeze. It materializes that a
battle has been raging around St. Hilarion Castle during my
sojourn in the marine mountains. The Greeks have captured
another peak and are within five hundred yards of the castle.
I drive up a precipitous road to the castle, awaiting with
trepidation a withering burst of Bren gun fire. It doesn't
come. The castle is absorbed in peace, sugar-cake battlements crumbling in the sun.

April 27.
I return to the castle and visit two middle-aged English
ladies who live in a bird sanctuary in the middle of the
mountain battlefield. They take me around the sanctuary
above Kyrenia making such observations as: 'That's a
Turkish position over there but the booms seem to have
moved over that way a bit.' They know every gun position
threatening their paradise where butterflies trip prettily
among flowers, olive and carob trees. I drive through
deserted villages, one of which the Turks have threatened to
annihilate by detonating the mountainside beside it. I
penetrate the castle this time and wander around its
beleaguered battlements. A notice states: 'Visitors 9am to
5pm.'

May 2.
Famagusta on a warm Saturday. I swim in clear waters, roll
luxuriously in warm sand, share enormous barbecued tunny
fish with five other journalists on the beach. We drive back
to Nicosia through the gathering dusk, through prairie fields
of corn with mountains retreating behind the mists of night.

A complex story in the village of Louridgine. Greeks have shot up a bus packed with old people and killed a Turk aged 60. The Turks believe the United Nations is sending an ambulance to pick up the body for a post mortem. Dusky little girls wait brandishing anti-UN and anti-Greek slogans; wait and wait — for two and a half hours. In the twilight depths of the mosque three girls, two boys and two soldiers stay beside the body. Anger replaces sorrow. UNO deny they ever promised an ambulance. A hot-head schoolmaster, convinced of pro-Greek bias, says his boys will go to the main road and shoot some Greeks to ensure that an ambulance is sent. UNO say they will send a helicopter to hold an inquiry: the helicopter never arrives. Another illustration of well-meant futility.

May 4.
A barbecue celebrating the Greek Easter Monday. I eat chunks of tough meat and crack brightly-painted eggs against eggs held by other guests — rather like conkers. A speaker says he hopes the tennis club where the barbecue is being held will be of assistance in achieving a peaceful solution in Cyprus. Less than half a mile away military police are investigating the attempted murder of two British soldiers. Two hand grenades were thrown at them while they were on patrol. One of the folk dances at the barbecue symbolises 'peace and happiness in the countryside'.

May 6.
I visit the Nicosia suburb of Trakhonas, a no man's-land of bungalows packaged with sandbags. The shuttered windows are spiked with guns, the gardens daubed with geraniums and creamed with roses. Earlier in the morning the Turks fired on Greeks building fortifications. Children were playing around the fortification and the Canadians with the UN wonder if they were planted there to stop the Turks shooting.

On to the village of Pyleri where Sherwood Foresters are sunbathing in the shadow of the Kyrenian mountains, crested with a coil of mist sliding down the hillside. The scene is incongruous, remote from war. A donkey regards me balefully and scrub-haired children thumb-suck their way behind me. The soldiers munch mess-tins of bangers.

I visit the French Canadians and find one major belligerently threatening to plaster a hill code-named Whisky with heavy machine-gun fire if the Greek Cypriots don't stop shooting in their direction. He also threatens to withdraw protective troops from two villages if the Turks don't withdraw a gun post. The gun post remains and the troops withdraw despite pleas from women and children in the two villages. Less than an hour later the troops are back again, the major's decision apparently counter-ordered. I lunch at the Harbour Club in Kyrenia overlooking the tranquil sea. As I drink asparagus soup truck-loads of police and arms scurry past.

May 7.
Days of relative inertia as fighting fades throughout the island. Have a few drinks at John Ogers with Jack Starr, canny Scot, meticulous journalist and accomplished pianist, from the *Daily Mail* and Harry Miller from the *Telegraph*. Although Harry is shorter than I we are often taken to be brothers − the same ridged hair, a shared funny bone. Once when we were driven blindfold to an Eoka Press conference a gun-toting guerilla announced: 'We are discussing hostages.' Harry and I both thought he said 'disgusting sausages'. As the *Telegraph* and the *Express* are not sworn enemies we work closely together; the competitive spirit only apparent when, whooping and sighing, we play our daily games of bar football in a café adjoining Murder Mile watched by lugubrious gunmen who have taken to betting on our results.

We leave John Ogers and wander down Regina Street, the Wardour Street of Nicosia. The little juke-box bars are full of Finns, Swedes, Austrian police, Greek-Cypriot Army and British soldiers, brown and hard, as ruthlessly witty as a football crowd. We play darts in the inevitable furnished imitation English pub. A Finn demands to be shown how to

94

play and throws the darts like javelins, grunting ferociously. Later have a drink in another bar where the Cypriot barmaids are both drunk. After each drink they hurl glasses and bottles on to the floor. A dazed Swedish journalist enters, dodges a hail of bottles and tells Harry Miller: 'You are a spy.' This excites the barmaids who expose their breasts.

May 8.
I drive to the airport to see off the Paras. Col. Pat Thursby, as dapper as the late Jack Buchanan despite camouflage flak-jacket and dusty boots; Major Mike Heerie, a handsome tough who looks 30 but is in fact 40. The usual vague sadness of parting which Harry and I attempt to drown later in the bar with the bottle-throwing barmaids. All quiet on the Cypriot Front.

May 11.
We all drive across the plain to Famagusta where three men are reported to have been shot dead. And dead they are. Apparently Costas Pantelides, son of the Nicosia police chief, took three Greek Army officers inside the walled city. They were gunned down reaching – according to the Turks – for their guns. Pantelides and two Greeks are dead; the third Greek is badly hurt; a Turk civilian also dies. Drying blood has spread around a British-style red telephone kiosk where the shooting took place.

The office of the Antiquities Bureau is opposite the kiosk. It is packed with Irish Army looking as tough as GIs in an American war film in the dough-boy blue UN helmets. They express anxiety at the consequences of the incident but their concern with death is minimal – they have come to terms with it.

We drive back to Nicosia through some of the toughest road blocks I have come across, lorries manned by Cypriots gazing thoughtfully through Bren gun sights. Mountains, dark and remote, vanish beneath castles of cloud and the sky is stained orange, then red.

May 12.

An extraordinary interview with the Greek officer who was
shot in Famagusta. He still has three bullets in him, one in
the chest and two in one leg. As he talks a doctor leans
across the bed to show us X-rays of the wounds, bullets
clearly marked. The officer claims they entered the walled
city by mistake. This is about as credible as the Turkish
claims that the Greeks were there to spy. You don't stray off
a main road and enter a gate in a walled city by mistake:
similarly you don't spy in broad daylight carrying identity
papers.

We visit the Turkish Information Office; its walls are
papered with photographs of alleged Greek atrocities –
bodies exhumed ten days after death, a child murdered in his
bath. Beside the photographs a girl of 14 or 15 sits typing
with sweet composure; the counterpart of a London typist
waiting for elevenses and postcards from the girls in Spain.

That evening Harry and I visit an Army camp to see the
Forces entertainment show with singer Lita Roza. She was
here when I first came to Cyprus for the *Daily Mirror* during
the Suez crisis in 1956. The stage: a cookhouse. Lita sings
sweetly and with passion apart from one moment when the
pianist falters. Backstage she admonishes him in a manner
not entirely unknown in Army cookhouses.

May 13.

My ankle has developed a mysterious and painful swelling.
An army doctor has it X-rayed, gives me pain-killing
injection and packs it with ice. The treatment has no
remedial effect whatsoever. My ankle hurts like hell but I
have become the clown of the outfit. Why are my complaints
always funny? First hay fever, now gout!

May 15.

Archbishop Makarios visits Famagusta to try and soothe
feelings and get hostages released. I drive ahead in the
snarling hornet of a car I have acquired – a red, open MG. I

96

take Jack Starr with me. The Archbishop, smiling secretly into his beard, tours the docks.

I drink a bottle of beer and chat with ABC cameraman, Joe Valetta. He looks like a Sicilian gangster – stocky, greying curly hair, swarthy, huge cigar, Bronx accent, swears like a stoker. And he always gets in front of other photographers. 'They get their pictures away foist,' he says. 'but the shmucks have only got pictures of my head.' They all hate him, he says, because 'I get more money than them'. We barbecue red mullet on the beach. On the road back, shimmering with mirages, I overtake Harry Miller in a new Cortina in my red flyer.

May 16.
Thunderstorms and the smell of wet dust. I drive to a beach seven miles from Kyrenia. Wild Spanish scenery, dark sand, white-tufted sea. Only two other people on the beach. Swim in the warm water. The rocks on the shore are scattered with scarlet poppies and mauve convolvulus. Lunch on the balcony of a faded hotel and throw bones to vulpine dogs who chase skinny cats from their scavenging fields.

May 18.
Drive to Limassol, a dusty little port cradling cargo ships in its arms. Drive through it to Ladies' Mile Beach where British families sprawl. Tents, pots of tea, baggy bathing costumes, transistors blaring, mothers herding sun-browned children, corned-beef lunches, menfolk reading yesterday's *News of the World* and holding monosyllabic conversations with freckled wives. It is Whit Monday. Lunch in the Metropole, a British-managed hotel filled with British families eating British food. *'I told the wife, we'd be better off in Blackpool . . . '* I drive back through the white foothills of the Troodos mountains, stumpy protuberances shaped like mammaries, boxes, pyramids, across the plain.

May 19.
I go on patrol with the Gunners inside the walled city of

97

Nicosia. Yesterday a grenade was hurled at them; they hurled themselves round a corner and so escaped death. I wander through dark streets with desperate nonchalance beside Sgt. Simpson and Gunner Dearnley. They chat with equal friendliness to their own colleagues lurking in doorways and Greek-Cypriots snuggling behind sandbags. Thin cats fight, starving dogs pad behind us; shutters swing to and fro eerily. Sergeant Simpson, a man of stoic good humour, was present when the Greek-Cypriots shot a nine-year-old boy. He had just given him a Mars bar. The Gunners have a trick up their sleeves: they post two coal-black Fijians who can hardly be seen at night in a doorway and, as the Greek-Cypriots wander past, they rattle the bolts of their rifles. The result is electrifying.

May 20.
Hard day writing a feature that will never be used. Pleasantly surprised to get a play cable telling me yesterday's story was splashed in the early editions. Adjourn for a drink and steak in the evening and get word very late that the inevitable has happened – a United Nations soldier has been killed. A Finn.

May 21.
Drive out to the village four miles from Nicosia where the Finn was shot. A poor parched hamlet surrounded by rustling cornfields. The Finns were attacked by Turkish-Cypriots. Both sides claim they challenged each other without result. The Turks say they thought the Finns were Greeks mounting an attack. Anyway, a young man who knew little of the problems of Cyprus – and probably cared even less – died in a foreign and alien land. Why? What chess master decided to transport a pawn from Finland to be murdered in this speck of land in the Mediterranean? He was the son of a high-ranking Finnish Army Officer. A British Army spokesman makes the fatuous comment: 'Soldiers expect to die.'

May 26.
Three outbreaks of shooting involving Canadians. Difficult
to see what the Cypriots' objective is unless it's merely to
keep the crisis boiling. In the morning Turkish-Cypriots
open fire with a Vickers machine-gun on Greeks being
escorted by Canadians to harvesting. In the afternoon
Greek-Cypriots open up on Swedish police being escorted
by Canadians. With them is an Italian TV and radio officer
attached to the UN. His car is shot up but he has the
presence of mind to keep his tape-recorder going. He plays
the tape in the bar in the evening and we hear the bullets
zipping around, smashing the windscreen and puncturing a
tyre. We hear a member of the Italian crew ask: 'Do you
think they've stopped?' The answer: a hail of bullets. In the
evening a Canadian jeep is shot at. Throughout the day
some 300 shots are fired — and no one is hurt.

May 27.
The jacaranda in the front garden of the Nicosia Palace
Hotel has misted into mauve bloom. Geraniums daub
gardens with blossom, a different flower indeed from the
spindly-legged geraniums of England. Roses, however,
don't have any fragrance. The temperature today touched 85
degrees and it is getting hotter, almost too hot to touch the
typewriter on my balcony. In the squares old men lazily
squeeze oranges into squash — 6d. a glass containing the
juice of seven or eight fruit; lolloping dogs sigh in warm
shade; Danes, Swedes and Finns sweat and dream of the
cold. And rival gunmen peer through their gun-sights and
caress their triggers.
    The Press is summoned to see the Interior Minister who
discloses that a young British aircraftsman has been arrested
and charged with smuggling arms to the Turks. It is alleged
that two mortars, frogmen's suits and 'seditious documents'
were found in his car. See the airman in court; he was
arrested with his wife and one-year-old baby boy. There are
extraordinary scenes while police remove handcuffs from
the young and dazed airman; photographers pile into the

99

courthouse while police stand back and allow the young couple to be humiliated. Jack Starr protests and the couple are led to the end of a corridor where their humiliation continues. I get the wife a chair, too late. They are led into court where the photography continues. The baby chuckles and gurgles; the airman protests that he has not been able to see anyone from the RAF to represent him. There is a noisy scene when I try to ask the baby's name: a police officer loses control of himself and screams hysterically.

May 28.
Searches are stepped up after the arms incident involving the airman. My MG is searched thoroughly. Police find a Turkish handout in the possession of an agency reporter and friend of mine, Jim Brown, and hold him at the roadside for ten minutes. In the afternoon a homely anti-British demonstration in 91 degrees. Crowds lick multi-coloured ice-creams and nod approvingly but without enthusiasm.

May 29.
Some 5,000 schoolchildren parade for the first lesson of the day: an anti-British demonstration. The boys wear white shirts and grey trousers; the girls blue uniforms and giggles. These were the sort of demonstrations in the '50s that preceded the Eoka campaign. How innocent are the catalysts of violence on this island?

June 7.
Cyprus is in the grip of a scare that the Turks are poised to invade from the mainland. I find it hard to believe. I drive by myself to Kyrenia and swim in the warm sea. Spurs of white cloud peer over the mountains, each the same shape as their respective peaks. The hills are dark and thoughtful. United Nations troops bathe on the dun-coloured beach, bees hover over small blue thistles. The island is changing colour; the greenery has been burned up to be replaced by desert hues. On the way back to Nicosia a thunderstorm overtakes me. I button up my red hornet and shelter in a Turkish café. Rain

100

sluices down and the air is sweet and acrid with the smell of water on dust. A lean dog tries to escape from the rain and howls at the door of his master's house; but no one takes any notice and he tries to hide behind a dustbin.

June 13.
The Queen's official birthday. I and several other reporters have already written a story about RAF officers objecting to an invitation to Archbishop Makarios and his Minister of the Interior to a reception at their mess. It really is a bizarre gesture when it is common knowledge that the wily prelate supports Eoka. We pool the story, excluding one reporter who rarely leaves the bar and survives by ear-wigging and picking the brains of young newcomers who are flattered to be in his august presence. It is our revenge, petty no doubt, for all those occasions when we have returned from a battlefield with the smell of death still in our nostrils to find him freshly groomed at the bar; worse, he's always filed while we have to ad-lib if we're lucky enough to get a line to London. But this time he is comprehensively screwed. He receives the inevitable late night why-you-unfiled call from London when the story appears in the early editions of the other papers and I find him in the bar peering darkly into his gin-and-tonic. I feel ashamed instead of elated. But he is a survivor: the following day he cables a story that the rumours about the reception have been officially denied. He regards this as an exclusive and chuckles from time to time as he peers optimistically once more into his crystal ball, a large G and T.

As the story about the officers' objections has been published I attend the reception with trepidation. Jolly girls prattle, medals jingle, minor Government officials volunteer: 'No comment, old man,' when you haven't asked them a question.

Makarios proposes the toast to the Queen. There is then an embarrassing pause of about a minute that seems like an hour. A little fellow beside me starts applauding but his handclaps peter away and he stares at his feet. The

101

Archbishop tentatively raises his glass of lemon squash; the High Commissioner, General William Bishop, steps forward belatedly and tries to explain the pause – he expected the Archbishop to make a speech as he did last year. A military band plays moodily in the corner, coiffures wilt. Happy birthday, ma'am!

June 19.
Recall 12 weeks after leaving England. There can't be many jobs where you go to work promising to try and be home early – there were kippers for supper that evening – and return three months later. I make a last tour of Nicosia. Old women are selling piles of cherries, as glistening black as caviar; the sky is deep blue, galleons of cloud on the horizon; the hot air quivers with insect noise. I play a last set of bar football with Harry Miller and win all three; unsmiling men who must have backed Harry tap the gun-bulges in their jackets irritably. I shall miss Harry, his exuberant laughter, his concertina trousers, his irreverence. And I shall miss walking the dogs with him – battery-powered, Japanese-made furry friends that we exercised outside the Ledra Palace every morning to the consternation of the staff. The august presence in the bar was heard to complain that we were letting the side down. Harry is, in fact, a superb craftsman, fast, accurate and intuitive and passionately loyal to the *Telegraph*; he also possesses an enviable sense of the ridiculous, machine-gunning sententious handouts to shreds with his typewriter.

Don Wise has returned so a good team will be assembled in my absence. He is 6ft. 4 inches tall, fiercely moustached, brown-baked, preposterously elegant. He once tossed a bruiser who mistook his sartorial splendour for effeteness across a bar with what appeared to be a roll of his wrist. He was once with the *Express*, but changed to the *Mirror*; a shame because his flamboyant style is cramped by a tabloid. Stories of his exploits have enlivened many a bibulous gathering. I like to think of him in his pre-journalistic days when he was in the Army fighting Malayan terrorists. The need for absolute quiet was impressed upon his platoon as it crept one night towards a farmhouse occupied by the enemy. And absolute quiet did prevail — until a duck with pro-terrorist sympathies grabbed Wise's balls in its beak.

I throw a small farewell party on the balcony of my room. The sky is deep with stars and the quarrels on this minuscule island on this tiny planet are a scarcely-heard discord in the chiming realms of space. Silhouetted on the roof of the hotel is a Danish soldier; his gun and his helmet are starkly etched but he has no face. I catch the 2.15am plane to London.

June 20.
In a few days' time we move house from Mitcham to Banstead. I vanish from civilisation among tea-chests, carpets, photographs, pieces of lawn-mower, legal documents, children, the cat, old shoes and spirited exchanges about what we should keep and what we should discard. I make furtive visits to the dustbin; Elizabeth makes equally furtive visits to retrieve what I have rejected.

July 9.
In our new home. The house is white with blue paintwork, becalmed among trees, mossy lawns, wild roses and a murky fishpond, crowned with tall chimneys. I lived in Banstead during the '40s in a semi-detached at 55 Salisbury Road, a steep hill that led coincidentally to Lambert Road, part of a council estate. I attended the Priory, a private school; the uniform was dark blue with pink piping, the cap looking like some exotic bloom, and it had an apoplectic effect on my contemporaries in Lambert Road; to reach home I had to dodge fusillades of stones, and four-letter words were frequently chalked on the pavement outside the house. I asked my mother what they meant and she said they were all connected with lavatories. Happily I subsequently discovered that the sexual act is not necessarily performed beneath a cistern.

Banstead was my war, a war taking a ten-year-old into his teens. Bomb craters, hot shrapnel, dried eggs and dried milk and national bread, sweet coupons, blue identity cards, stirrup pumps, Wailing Winnie − the air-raid siren, armadas of planes fighting it out in summer skies, Doodle-bugs − V2 rockets, Betty Grable and Will Hay, the Varga Girls of *Esquire*, *Health and Beauty* illustrated with girls with no pubes, Jane in the *Daily Mirror*, serving King and country in the Air Training Corps at Epsom College, learning French from a master there rumoured to have had his backside shot off in World War I, digging potatoes, cycling to the Priory one day to discover it in flames − a schoolboy's dream come true, compliments of the enemy. I put it all down in *The Sheltered Days*.

I spend a week at the Old Bailey on a wonderful fraud. A gang has taken a tobacconist for a ride − with cement balls. One posing as a Russian peasant strode into his shop, cracked open a cement ball and out popped a gold sovereign. It so happened that there was a French customer present who translates Russian − another member of the gang. The peasant continued to crack cement balls, each containing sovereigns, until they were ready for the big tickle. The tobacconist agreed to buy several thousand cement balls for £1,500. They took his money − then handed it back while they went to fetch the rest of the balls. They have, in fact, switched the packets of banknotes and they do not return. The tobacconist is left with a wad of paper and several cement balls containing nothing but cement.

July 11.
Take the boys to Betchworth to see the *Daily Mail* v *Daily Express* cricket match. An apple-green ground, surrounded by graceful trees that sigh in the breeze adjoining a pub selling good nutty beer. What more could you want on a soft summer day? Much of the pleasure is anticipatory: seeing Harry Benson, my Glaswegian partner, bat. We arrive to see him skulking near the sight-screen in flannels that the house painter must have left behind, and suede shoes. The

Express win easily with the help of a free-lance who plays for a Shropshire League Club. The *Express* once played Keith Miller who writes for them; a top-class, club-standard fast bowler said it was like bowling at a barn door, and a barn door that swung!

July 14.
End up after midnight interviewing a small bull at the end of a munched-up lawn in Shepherds Bush. The owner, Frank Shapiro, aged 21, has to get rid of it because it eats his father's roses and chases his mother up the garden at 30mph. Frank is flying to Israel to get a job in beef production. To prepare himself he bought the calf, named Noddy, and built an inflatable stable. Says Frank, who emerges in his pyjamas: 'I've got to get rid of Noddy because of Dad and the next-door neighbour. She says he smells. But I'm sure Dad's got a soft spot for Noddy.' Dad declines to comment. Who can blame him at this time of night?

July 15.
A day off in my new domain. Settled in now but still banging up shelves and hiding suitcases in the loft. I attend open day at Martin's new school. Poor Martin, apparently he is behind the other children in English. A beautiful school with large airy classrooms, bright paint and special smiles for parents.

July 17.
News breaks that the washing-machine empire of John Bloom has crashed. He cut prices by cutting out the middle man and selling direct to housewives. Drive to Finchley to see one of his directors, a Mr Jack Jacobs. Mission unsuccessful. Return across Hampstead Heath. The pubs are crowded with shirt-sleeved men and brown girls drinking warm beer and shandy; they ooze out into courtyards and gardens beneath bright umbrellas advertising apéritifs. I see the scene photographed and frozen and displayed in fifty

105

years' time; just as today we see Edwardian boaters above damp forelocks and girls with high-piled curly hair in long striped dresses.

July 19.
On with the Bloom story. I drive to his Park Lane flat to await his return from the Continent. Passers-by see the Press waiting outside and wait for they know-not-what just as people joined queues in the last war.

July 23.
Tottenham Hotspurs' football ground, White Hart Lane. Two days ago Scottish international John White was killed by a flash of lightning sheltering under a tree on a golf course. A poignant experience standing on the desolate, out-of-season terraces as the Spurs observe a minute's silence. I am struck by how unhealthy those engaged in sporting activity appear. Strained, over-trained faces.

August 2.
My parents are inspecting the new house, expecting me home on my day off tomorrow, when I return to announce that I have to go to Jersey where there has been another outbreak of sex crimes. At St. Helier airport I meet Sid Williams of the *Herald* and Owen Summers of the *Sketch* and we interview Supt. James Axon and his sergeant on the terrace of our seafront hotel.

August 3.
Hire a blue MG Midget — memories of Cyprus — but find the charms of St. Helier elusive. It is packed, the beaches are dirty and the air smells of rotting seaweed. Its bars are shabby, beer-stained and paint-cracked; its gift shops predictably tawdry; and yet it basks in an unwarranted glow of sophistication. Give me the honestly vulgar fish-and-chip charms of Brighton or Southend any day. We meet Axon again at the police station. Cups of tea all round and minimal information. 'Just spade work,' says Axon. 'Checking and

re-checking.' This is the fifteenth time a woman or a young person has been sexually assaulted in Jersey in the past few years. The last victim was a 16-year-old boy. 'A shy boy,' says Axon. The assailant entered his room, told him his parents would be 'got at' if he didn't do what he was told and assaulted him in a nearby field. What incalculable harm must have been done to that 'shy boy'. A local police officer says: 'Don't interview any of my men − I don't want personalities mentioned.' He tells us about last week's battle of flowers and advises us about the best places to eat.

August 7.
Austria for a holiday. Swissair to Zurich, nosing through alpine valleys, land in teeming rain. By train to Zell-am-Zee, then decrepit bus to Saalbach. The mountains are sheathed with cloud and the village reminds me a little of Klosters without the snow, wealth and health.

I went to Klosters several years ago for the *Mirror* when the 21-year-old Duke of Kent's name was linked with a pretty 18-year-old deb named Jane Sheffield. He kissed her at the railway station and THE KISS spanned a page of the *Mirror*. In fact at that period when Princess Margaret's name was being wildly linked with Prince Bertil of Sweden − her ill-fated romance with Peter Townsend had earlier foundered − Royalty only had to sneeze to merit half a column. Uninvited I accompanied the Duke and his Society friends on a ski-ing expedition to the top of a mountain. They were all casually elegant; I wore a mail-order sweater, the trousers of my suit, and hired skis that looked like floorboards. My initiative was further jeopardised by the fact that I couldn't ski. I approached the Duke, introduced myself chummily and announced that I was the Man from the *Mirror*. His reply was succinct, the second word being *off*. He and his party then launched themselves down the mountainside. At this moment the chair-lift stopped. Dusk was settling, mist rising, snow falling. I buckled on my floorboards and skied into a tree. I heard a resounding crack and assumed I had broken a leg; in fact it

107

was the stem of my bulldog pipe in my trousers' pocket. I arrived at the hotel hours later to find the Duke and his party relaxing in an *après-ski* glow.

August 9.
Trouble has again broken out in Cyprus. Turkish planes have been strafing Greek-Cypriots, many dead or wounded. I feel I should be there and feel guilty that I do.

August 12.
We chair-lift to the top of a small mountain. The air smells sweet and sharp as we rise sedately, leaving behind pencil-point pines and the village kneeling at the foot of the green, onion-dome church. At the top a view of snow-crested peaks as remote as stars. We climb down through pines, their branches dripping with beards of moss. The skeletal limbs of dead trees make an abandoned battlefield of the spongy ground. Then we burst into open grassland drying in the sun. Butterflies flirt, the turf is embroidered with harebells; armies of grasshoppers jump before our clumsy feet, the air is alive with their busy noise and the tinkling of distant cowbells.

August 13.
Bus to Zell-am-Zee. Cream cakes beside the ruffled lake. In the distance a snow-dusted range of mountains. We take out a rowing boat and paddle past deep hillsides and grey beaches. Plump Germans and Austrians and their plump wives and plump children promenade under the linden trees. Once more I feel the chocolate box prettiness of Klosters arranged for the photographer. 'A little to the left, Mr Mountain. That's better. Just one more.'

Was this the atmosphere that pervaded Austria and Germany in 1939? An amalgam of unwavering belief in their supremacy, whipped-cream health and complacency? The hindsight feeling was strong last night when we had a Tyrolean evening at the hostel. Foaming beer, loud silly dances, flatulent good humour. They could have been celebrating the declaration of war as the last step towards final victory.

August 14.
Walking through pine woods, damming a stream, dodging down the hills, returning to the hostel for a beer, another of those lunches served on a platter with compartments for the vegetables, a game of mini-golf . . . Patrick swims in the icy water of the village pool, then we adjourn to the little cinema to see a British 'Carry-on' film but we are turned away because the children are too young. We shall never see a movie in Austria!

August 16.
We eat large ice-creams clotted with cream, drink non-alcoholic apple-juice, photograph wild flowers in colour. Elizabeth has refused to ascend in the chair-lift so our walks are now upwards. In the afternoon and evening torrential rain falls and thunder rolls around the mountains trying to escape. The last liquid light is disappearing behind the peaks, and clouds, soft and inky, are gathering between them. All today, a Sunday, the church bells have been chiming and the men have been parading in their old, soap-pressed suits and Tyrolean hats waiting for the ghost of Ivor Novello to set them to music.

August 17.
A bright blue day and we take the cable car up the Schattberg and walk across a spine of peaks dipping through starved grassland. In the distance snow-capped ranges of mountains, including the Grossglöckner, spike the quiet sky. Elizabeth rides in the cable car staring steadfastly at her feet. In the afternoon we sunbathe at the pool and Patrick bathes once more in the icy, sky-coloured water.

August 18.
A blue Mercedes, driven by a pleasant young Austrian who once fractured his spine racing cars, picks us up at 7am to

take us to Berchtesgaden and Salzburg. We drive to a café overlooking Berchtesgaden and facing the Eagle's Nest where Hitler plotted and played and brooded. Twenty-five years ago I was on parade on a station platform at Muswell Hill and evacuated from my parents because of his machinations, although at the time we paid him scant respect, brushing our hair over our foreheads, charcoaling moustaches and heiling between explosions of mirth. There, near the top of that pretty mountain overlooking Berchtesgaden — from here each green roof looks like a tile — one man planned war, genocide and grinding misery unequalled in the evolution of our species. Was he there when I toddled off to that alien land known as the country? Was he there as all those mothers sobbed farewells to their children and wondered if they would ever see them again? And where is he now? The driver is reluctant to discuss the Führer. He tells Elizabeth, 'My father was a Nazi.'

On across the border to Salzburg. Elizabeth feels dizzy as we tramp the streets cobbled with tourists so we take the funicular to the castle which does nothing to improve her dizziness. We munch our rolls and drink beer and gaze over the river, the crotchets and quavers of musical old buildings, the new blocks breaking up the tranquil skyline. Back to Salzburg and cold rain.

August 22.
Another grey drizzle of a day to anti-climax the holiday. We've had a lot of laughs, a lot of sunshine. But the monotony of mountains — and the food — becomes oppressive after a week. Last evening meal not improved by Martin's discovery of a fly in his salad. Doubt if we will choose Austria again. I become irritated, too, with the noise of the French and Germans, particularly a group who take over the football game in the bowling alley. They turn out to be British!

September 1.
A journey into the past. Back along the A1 to St. Neots and

then to Abbotsley where 25 years ago I was evacuated. I knock at the door of the white semi-detached house where I ate, fought and cried with huge enthusiasm, but there is no reply. The village has not changed; the village green where I first espied my father on one of his visits is still neatly sewn into the middle of the straw-bonneted cottages; there is the cricket ground with its freshly-harvested pitch where leg breaks turned at right angles. The pond with its carpet of weed has dried up; and the inside of the pub − once so adult and secret − is a disappointment with its ordinary tables and beer mats advertising various brews. I find my first foster mother, Mrs Storey, staying with her mother on the outskirts of St. Neots. I remember her as pale with straight hair: she now has roseate cheeks and curly hair touched with grey. She remembers me as the more strident of her two charges and says that I was not always kind to my companion, a boy named Kenneth Francis. My memory is that, by rubbing his heels on the bottom of a zinc bath, he simulated gargantuan farting, then blamed me. In retaliation I threw his underpants out of the bedroom window. I remember the long garden filled with vegetables that I thought only materialised in greengrocer's and the sweet-grassed meadow at the end of it and the smirking children waiting to punish the cockney kids for their intrusion and the shack at the end of the garden where we did our business without chain or cistern and the air-raid drill in case the Jerries singled out Abbotsley for destruction. And whipping tops and a girl from Hornsey who cried incessantly and the visits from my parents armed with Wrights' Coal Tar Soap and comics and Ex-lax, and thick woods that swallowed our shouts and the Storeys' dog, a black and white clown called Toby, and a schoolmistress named Miss Kenyon with whom I had been in love for many months. But really all I wanted in those embryonic days of the war was brown bread and gooseberry jam on Sunday afternoons with yellow London fog rolling up to the windows of our house in The Chine in Muswell Hill.

I write a feature about the visit for the *Express*.

111

September 2–10.
A few dreary days at the Old Bailey. A hotel thief who had himself a ball in Paris after stealing travellers' cheques from big London hotels; a gang who snatched jewels from a Bond Street shop. Then a trip to Cobham, Kent, where gypsies, emphatically unromantic, are being evicted; the trip is relieved by a pint in a pub where Dickens was supposed to have drunk.

The following day I drive into Hampshire, taking Patrick, to look for a puma said to be terrorising the district. The village is divided. Some say: 'It's just some old pussy cat.' Others insist: 'It's a fearsome beast.' I make the mistake of treating the affair with levity in front of one of the latter. His wife says: 'I hope you meet him on a dark night.' They also have a large Alsatian straining at the leash which looks as if it would also like to meet me after dusk. Or before it for that matter.

September 14.
I ask if I can take over articles about the open-air life and adventure. I begin by going to a quarry in Kent with Patrick to find fossils. The quarry is a petrified, tranquil place where life stirred beneath the sea 85 million years ago. It is littered with iron nodules as smooth as cricket balls, fool's gold and ammonites, lamellibranchs and belemnites – slender, amber-coloured relics like the tips of knitting needles.

September 15.
I hear that my book about a childhood in the last war, *The Sheltered Days*, is to be published. Celebrate in the Victoria, a pub in Banstead, with Elizabeth.

September 19.
We drive to Biggin Hill to see the Battle of Britain air display. Faster-than-sound planes like red and yellow darts scream through the skies; old biplanes lumber flatly into view. A Spitfire – perhaps the most beautiful aircraft ever

designed – whips around followed by a Hurricane. In a hangar we view Messerschmitt 109s and Heinkel 111s, once the sinister symbols of destruction observed and recorded by young plane-spotters before they dived into Anderson shelters as ack-ack fire blossomed in the sky.

September 21.
Catch a train to Dover on my way to meet Dr. Petrucci, who claims to be able to create human life from the ovum of a woman and the sperm of a man. Coffee outside Dunkirk station. I try and visualise the scenes nearly a quarter of a century ago when the British Army was evacuated from the jaws of the Wehrmacht. I am driven in a Citroën through waking villages to Calais. Early morning smells sneak in through the windows and the driver tells us he has been driving taxis for 35 years: he should know the road by now. I arrive with photographer Stan Meagher at Calais far too early to meet the doctor off a train from Milan. Finally he arrives, neat-bearded, articulate and proud of his claims. We drink tea on the Channel ferry and he tells me that he is convinced that it is possible to 'manufacture' a baby in a laboratory. I shield him from a couple of Pressmen at Folkstone and hire an old London taxi to London to avoid the opposition at Victoria Station.

September 25.
A woman who has spent 21 of the past 25 years in prison appeals against a sentence for stealing a raincoat from a store. Her counsel describes how the woman, who has a 'delightful speaking voice', has started recording textbooks for the blind and realises how much better off she was than many other people. Her character, hitherto hostile to authority, has softened, he says. She has a gaunt face brightened by touches of make-up and a flicker of hope. The judges allow her appeal; I hope their mercy flourishes.

October 1.
Collect the woman who has started making recordings for

113

the blind and, with Harry Benson, I take her to Hampstead Heath for photographs — back view only. She tells me about life in prison, the grey hopelessness of Holloway in 1939; now, she says, there is hope. Prison reform has at last reached women's prisons. But, she tells me, women still leave jail without learning any trade — 'Girls don't even know how to cook on a bed-sitter ring.' She adds: 'I wouldn't have reformed before this. My character was all wrong, hard and bitter. It's only now that I'm ready for this sort of life.'

October 2.

Workers at the Hardy Spicer motor component factory in Birmingham are on strike and Harold Wilson alleges that the strike has been engineered by the Tories as an electioneering ploy. His reasoning is a little difficult to follow. I visit Herbert Hill, the company chairman, at his offices in Mayfair. He is a big, bulky man with a soft voice. While I am there he speaks to a news agency on the phone and describes the workers as 'poor dears' with little intelligence; his words are picked up by every newspaper in the land. He puts down the phone and says to me: 'I don't think I should have said that but it's true you know.' I agree with him that he should not have said it.

October 6.

Down to London Airport for the Queen's departure to Canada. There have been threats of assassination by French Canadian extremists but she seems remarkably calm about them. Home early still hugging the knowledge that my book has been accepted for publication.

October 7.

The last performance of the lunchtime radio show *Workers' Playtime*, which has been on the air for ever. At a corrugated case factory in Hatfield I chat with the compère, Bill Gates, who confides that he detests canteens and canteen food. A buoyant man of 48 — who insists that photographers do not take his picture when he is wearing spectacles. 'For the very last time, welcome to *Workers' Playtime* . . . ' Wild applause − but no stamping of feet or whistling by request of Mr Gates. He tells me that he cut out jokes about the works foreman. On the last show: Ann Shelton and Cyril Fletcher, whom I remember on the radio when we lived in Muswell Hill before the war. He recites an *odd ode* about a girl called Nellie who got stuck in a bath of jelly. Ann Shelton, perhaps the best of all the pop singers, sings. Then it's all over for ever.

October 8.
A gas explosion in a house in Brixton. I knock on doors waiting for the inevitable. A woman in curlers provides it. 'It was just like the Blitz,' she says. Another regular: 'He was a man who kept himself to himself,' referring to arsonists, bigamists and mass-murderers. But I suppose the most common quote is: 'Don't quote me but . . . ' followed by horrendous and libellous allegations.

The most unfortunate quotes I ever recorded were provided by a medical officer of health when, after National Service in the RAF, I had been working on the *Dartmouth Chronicle*, my first paper, for nine months. He told me that a case of smallpox had been admitted to Dartmouth Hospital. I immediately flogged the story to the national papers using the name Sellar-Hay who was the *Chronicle*'s editor and Fleet Street's local correspondent. I bought all the papers at Paignton railway station on my way to work and discovered that the story was on all the front pages. Ecstasy. Alighting at Dartmouth I met the medical officer who casually remarked: 'That smallpox, by the way, turned out to be chicken-pox.' Sellar-Hay, a rotund, acerbic Scot who made munching noises when he was irked, was waiting for me at the *Chronicle*'s ramshackle offices munching ferociously. And, although he would undoubtedly have been displeased if I hadn't taken the opportunity of making us some pocket money *if* the story had been true, sacked me on the spot. It was my 21st birthday.

October 12.

Take the train to Doncaster where Macmillan is speaking and occupy the compartment next to him. I notice the bowed figure of Macleod making his way along the corridor; he sits at the opposite end of it. I tell each of them that the other is on the train. They meet briefly and, perhaps, reluctantly. A rough time from the organised hecklers has been forecast for Macmillan. I tackle him about them and he says: 'What hecklers? I've heard nothing of them. Makes it all the easier, really – I don't have to speak too much.'

Macmillan receives a terrible bullying from vocal young louts. He deals with them adequately but he is not the same majestic orator he was before his operation. Anthony Barber, the Health Minister, is a fighting cock, though, and leaps to his feet to shout: 'I've never come across such behaviour in Doncaster before.' It's as exciting as the Cup Final.

October 15.

Election Day. It looks as if Labour will make it with a small majority – I have a bet on the Tories. Great excitement in the office and I linger until 2am as the results chatter over the teleprinters. The computers calculate that Labour will have a majority of between 25 and 30. At times like this a newspaper office lives up to its movie image. Teams of journalists compile and compute and drink coffee as the results are chalked in appropriate colours on a blackboard; pages are revamped; sub-editors lick their pencils with adrenalin.

October 16.

Labour in with a forecast majority of 4. It will do the Tories good – their leaders were becoming caricatures; nevertheless I wonder if Wilson and Brown are leaders of men. I see Wilson briefly in the glare of TV floodlights outside No.10 and have a word with Callaghan. He is asked by a reporter if he is pleased: he says he is: so much for the art of interviewing.

116

October 31.
The Surrey countryside is rich and sullen and smokily fragrant. We lunch in Dorking and then drive up Box Hill and play breathless (for me) football and walk in the woods behind the hill. I can't recall autumn hues ever being so vivid, yellow, bronze, crimson; delicate and translucent among the beech trees.

November 4.
A new clock is unveiled above Fortnum and Mason. A pretty thing in bronze and green on which the figures of the store's founders emerge every hour. The ceremony is watched by Field Marshal Lord Montgomery and newspaper proprietors Lord Thomson of Fleet and Cecil King. Afterwards a cold buffet and champagne: the Press adjourn for a quick one in Jules' Bar.

November 5.
Fireworks in a garden large enough at last for a bonfire. Guy Fawkes somehow marks the passing of the years more definitively than Christmas or Easter. Two years since I was in India. Or is it three?

December 10.
The diary has lapsed because I have been too busy experimenting with sequels to *The Sheltered Days* and trying to find a new job in television. The latter is half-hearted because I believe the pen to be mightier than the box but I am suffering from a bad attack of not-being-appreciated. From *Dartmouth Chronicle* to *Eastern Daily Press* in King's Lynn to *The Star* in Sheffield, *Daily Mirror* in Manchester and London, *Daily Express* (a raise of £2 a week) as general reporter then nothing. The next step should be a foreign posting but it hasn't materialised. I suffer, I think, from an ability journalistically to be able to turn my hand to anything. Or perhaps word of the long-ago smallpox fiasco has finally reached the hierarchy; certainly falling down the

117

stairs of Lyons' tea-shop in Ludgate Circus after consuming several schooners of sherry at the opening of a bar can't have helped my cause — a modest compensation was the expressions on the faces of the customers munching bath-buns and supping tea as I landed among them.

December 12.
Kenya becomes a republic within the Commonwealth with Jomo Kenyatta, once described as 'a leader unto darkness and death', or something like that, as the first president. I was among those present when he gave a Press conference at a transitional camp between internment by the British and eventual freedom. He displayed immense presence, humour and acumen and, although I hadn't experienced the ritual atrocities of Mau Mau, I felt then that this was the man to lead Kenya to stability and prosperity. The Press conference was also memorable for our transport to the camp in the hills; we all chartered small planes from Wilson airport and the sky was crowded with Red Barons and Biggles.

1965

January 24.
Sir Winston Churchill, the greatest Englishman of our time, perhaps all time, died today. I report to Hyde Park Gate at 10am. A huddle of people, mostly Pressmen, are gathered at the end of the cul-de-sac, besieged for nine days, leading into Kensington Gore. I, like everyone else, treasure my evocation of Churchill. For me it is the voice, swaggering, sardonic and steely, summoning me as a child from the garden in the sunlit summers of the war. Vapour trails lace the sky, the stirrup pump sprays wilting lettuce, an air-raid siren moans fretfully. I join my parents beside the wireless and listen to him snarling defiance at Herr Hitler and the 'Narzis'. He was an alchemist of words who burnished us ordinary people with the golden glow of patriotism. It is not difficult for an adult to strike awe into a child: it is a miracle to inspire devotion. Churchill performed this miracle with his Victory Vs, his colossal nerve, his voice which transformed a classroom into an embattled outpost. He was the greatest man we kids had ever encountered. The children of today are the poorer that they never knew his voice in those Spitfire summer days that are now history.

January 28.
The queue to see the coffin containing the body of Sir Winston Churchill in Westminster Hall is nearly two miles

long. Lots of sheepskin jackets, mostly women and girls. They seem bright and eager this grey morning as they wait and wonder if snow will fall. I climb to the top of the Fire Brigade building with Ron Dumont to watch the queue snaking along Millbank, over Lambeth Bridge, back along the Albert Embankment. Inside the hall I contemplate the catafalque and try to comprehend that therein lies the muted voice of war and victory.

The queue nudges me and I emerge into the dusk with a gaggle of schoolgirls.

January 29.
The eve of Churchill's funeral. I visit Patrick Gordon-Walker, the ex-Foreign Secretary who resigned after two humiliating election defeats. He is moving from the official residence back to his Hampstead home. A quiet, crumpled man bitterly hurt by his rejection. What upsets him most, he says, is the suggestion that he was defeated because he is aloof. His wife says: 'Aloof is absolutely the last word to describe Patrick. The children around here love him.' But they would not be able to vote for him. Although the ill-fitting suit, working-lad image of a Labour politician is fading, I still find it hard to relate the sort of house Mr Gordon-Walker inhabits with the ideals of socialism: it was up for sale for more than £20,000.

January 30.
Fly to Mozambique where fighting and arrests have been reported. Explore Lisbon en route and have a beer in the Suica in Rosis Square while cold rain sweeps pedestrians past its warm mouth. Joined by Dan Slater, with whom I once worked on the *Mirror*. We visit a couple of bars and return to the airport. The plane is delayed for an hour, then I manage to sleep till Luanda. I chat to a coffee planter and his middle-aged sun-ravaged wife; she has a tic in one eye and I am scared that her husband will see her winking at me; I do not wink back.

On from Salisbury by Constellation to Lourenco Marques;

but by this time I suspect that the story is exaggerated. LM, as the locals call it, is built around wide avenues hemmed with flame trees. I cross the road from my hotel to see the British consul, Mr Brian Heddy, a quiet, very white man with hidden reserves of humour which occasionally erupt. Apparently the PIDE – Portuguese CID – have made some arrests and the terrorism on the northern border continues, but reports of shooting and tension in LM *are* exaggerated. I phone Lindsay Smith in Johannesburg and manage to get a story out by chatting conversationally with him – if you try to dictate copy you are cut off.

February 1.
Take a look round LM. All is peaceful in this the capital city of a slice of one of the last colonial empires in the world, the Soviet Union excepted. I am told that blacks and whites mix freely, but I see little evidence of it. It's all very British with lots of Minis charging around on the left-hand side of the road. The Hotel Polana stands by the sea: it has a swimming pool where one might have expected creamy Roman maidens to besport themselves. Alas, no maidens of any nationality.

February 2.
Fly north with a Mr da Souza, the Portuguese information officer. He is incredibly solicitous; but I have no doubt that I will see only what I am supposed to see. We touch down finally at Porto Amelie. On the plane I interview, with the assistance of the air hostess, the governor of the northern territory where terrorists are on the attack, a natty little man who looks sharp and tough when I see him later in his lieutenant-colonel's uniform.

I am driven around the little town by the Portuguese administrator, who wears a starched white uniform and languidly acknowledges the salutes of Africans, who fall over themselves to doff their hats. It seems like a pantomime of colonial rule: but it isn't. The administrator speaks little English, I speak no Portuguese. We take drinks on the verandah of his house overlooking the crumpled waters of the bay. He has five children and a pleasant, plump wife who speaks no English. Why should she? We dine at a utility restaurant where, he assures me, we will see Africans dining with whites; we see none. But I do not doubt that relations are easier than in Rhodesia or South Africa where they have their own rigid solution. Spend the night alone in the governor's beach house, surrounded, I suspect, by terrorists.

February 3.
Inarticulate farewells before boarding a DC-3, disembark when the hostess explains: 'We cannot find the starter.' Finally away, bush, swamp and jungle looking like lichen that can be rubbed away with the thumb.

February 4.
Fly off to Johannesburg after much hand-shaking with Mr da Souza. Drive through the suburbs to the Langham Hotel in the centre of town. It is like a hot August day in England. The buildings are baby skyscrapers, the shops beneath a mixture of the opulent and tawdry. A sawn-off New York.

Wealth is extravagantly displayed and the Africans look better off than they do in many a former colony. The talk in the men-only bars is rough and naive. I like the wide streets that dip down the hill into pink vistas in the dusk. There are lots of beautiful girls abroad and they seem all the more beautiful because of their tanned skins and blonde hair. I feel very pallid.

February 5.
Flying orders. Back to London tonight. The whole affair has taken just a week and covered heaven knows how many thousands of miles. My pleasure at returning is there as always but this time it is tempered by a reluctance to continue living in cramped surroundings after this expansive vision of grassland, sunshine and farmhouses where, with massive arrogance, the inhabitants await the inevitable rebellion.

122

March 9.

The diary has lapsed again. The culprits: the beginning of a second precocious volume of autobiography about my National Service and domestic uncertainty – a friend on the Foreign Desk told me casually that I am going to be the permanent *Express* staffman in the Far East. But no official confirmation although I hover close to the foreign enclave on the far side of the editorial floor and wander nonchalantly in the path of the Foreign Editor, David English. The assignment would be daunting because the Vietnam story is gathering momentum – Lyndon Johnson has announced that America will continue 'actions that are justified as necessary for the defence of South Vietnam' and yesterday 3,500 marines landed in the south. So why haven't I received the summons? Perhaps word has reached David English of my exploits at bar football in Murder Mile.

The new book progresses fitfully between periods of despondency and elation. I think it may amuse; it may even have some sociological and historical value. What effect did two years enforced military service in a time of peace have on my generation? It certainly disciplined me and enabled me to break out of the eggshell of my upbringing – my neighbour in the Nissen hut at RAF Padgate carried a cut-throat razor in his sock. Another such neighbour, a red-haired cockney, awoke every morning at 6am on the dot at Tangmere in Sussex, farted explosively and announced inexplicably: 'The cat's pissed on the strawberries.' I taxed him with this but he merely smiled an enigmatic Fu Manchu smile. National Service also taught me the arts of skiving and scrounging and introduced me to the extraordinary linguistic variations of the verb to fuck.

My RAF career was unmemorable, getting off to an uneasy start when, on my first night, I tried to desert – I called home from a telephone in a hangar and told my father I was catching the next train south, but a fiercely-moustached flight-sergeant standing behind me thought otherwise – and went into a sharp decline, when as a medical orderly, I nearly killed the officer at RAF Chivenor, in Devon, with the punishing dose of sal volatile. I was discharged with the rating *good* which was tantamount to branding me an incorrigible rogue. But I did enjoy drill and I did discover camaraderie and I did study journalism and shorthand. It was a pity that I drove the ambulance through the rear wall of the sick quarters' garage.

While I hover in limbo world news takes curious twists. As America and Russia continue to race each other into space the British occupy themselves with dusty death. A child's body discovered in a coffin in Stepney last December is identified as Lady Anne Mowbray who died in 1481 aged nine; the remains are reinterred in Westminster Abbey. On March 3 the remains of Roger Casement are taken from Pentonville Prison and reburied in Dublin.

March 10.
I get the summons. Africa, not the Far East!

May 3.
Time to reflect on my new home-town. Salisbury is a spacious geometric city turreted in the centre with sawn-off skyscrapers. Dry heat quivers in its broad canyons; trees bloom languidly; smart shops beckon coolly: whites and blacks walk the hot pavements as though neither exists. The white men are sturdy-thighed, freckled and defensive; the blacks remote in their tattered clothes. The whites call the blacks munts.

I am staying in the old-fashioned Ambassador Hotel across the trees and picnicking Africans in Cecil Square from the more illustrious Meikles. Visiting MPs from Britain and assorted nosey-parkers stay in Meikles and the restaurant is as clean and crisp as a salad. But it does have a rough old bar at the back – men only and a Scottish barmaid – where we play dice.

I work in the office of a news agency run by Jim Biddulph, resolutely pale despite the sun, and Ronnie Legge, greying with a small, busy beard; both highly professional. They possess Telex, the answer to every reporter's prayers. If I were ever asked what is a foreign correspondent's most valuable asset I would answer: 'A flair for communications.' What is the use of a world scoop in the Rann of Kutch if you can't get the story out? Peter Younghusband, the *Daily Mail*'s gigantic staffman in Africa, is one of the best communications men in the game. When Younghusband eases his frame into the lavatory beware: he's probably got a carrier pigeon in there. Dan McGeachie of the *Express* once tried to file from some embattled city but, every time he tried to dictate, the telephone operator cut him off; he eventually managed to phone one or two words to *Express* men all over the world; they dispatched the words to London and a composite story was put together. That's communications.

Here the peril is a certain reporter who lurks behind the two Telex machines while you are transmitting. I conspire with an agency reporter to send me a phoney message: CONGRATULATIONS GREAT EXCLUSIVE STOP HOLDING TILL MONDAY. That was on Saturday and throughout Sunday the lurker haunted me and spoiled what would have been a perfectly good weekend.

The election takes place in four days. An historic poll in which Ian Smith and his Rhodesian Front party will almost certainly have their call for independence echoed through-out the electorate. But what electorate? That, of course, is the nerve within the aching tooth. Majority rule as champ-ioned by the Labour Government in Britain or continuing white supremacy. I am my usual ambivalent self. I can understand the progeny of Cecil Rhodes wanting to preserve what they have accomplished. Why should they sacrifice the life-style they have sculpted? The tobacco and the coal and the gold and the servants. 'Look what happened in the Congo,' they justifiably argue. Equally I can sympathise with the blacks living in council-house rows of inflated allotment huts outside Salisbury. But are villagers living in the wilderness really ready to vote? Why the hell not? Compromise, I regretfully conclude. A slow but inexorable progression to a responsible franchise.

My book, *The Sheltered Days*, which I wanted to call *The Shrapnel Days*, is to be published on June 18. But I shan't be in England for the launch. Launch . . . What do they mean by that? Chuck it in the harbour? I have decided to call the sequel *The Skiving Days*, the military career of 3111805 A.C.2. Lambert. I read a couple of the opening sequences:-
The First FFI (free from infection).

We queued in a hut wearing vests and goose pimples and clinging to our trousers.

'When it's your turn raise your arms and drop your trousers,' barked a starch-straight corporal.

'Not much choice if we raise our arms, is it?' remarked a bow-legged Welshman, valley voice climbing a mountain and returning.

'Do you want to be on a fucking charge, laddie?' the corporal demanded.

Shoulder blades moved like embryo wings, biceps bunched in fighter's arms, muscles flickered in thin white limbs, chests bulged beneath mats of hair, chests retreated in sad hollows. Giants and jockeys, we waited to expose ourselves like a regiment of flashers on Hampstead Heath.

After the exposure the corporal eyed me beadily and said: 'Clean as a whistle, eh, laddie?' adding in the new language I was learning: 'Watch where you dip your wick and maybe it'll stay like that.'

The Booklet. It was called *A Guide for Airmen on joining the RAF* and it contained a lot of mysterious advice. For instance: 'Do all your work in good heart and good spirit; determined to make the best of the job. The dull jobs are just as important as those more thrilling.' Polishing bedsprings just as important as flying a Meteor across a summer sky?

'Last word of general advice: If you feel, at any time, that you have a *genuine grievance* apply for an interview with your commanding officer and the grievance will be investigated and put right if it is a genuine one.' Thus encouraged, I complained that our hut was cold and the corporal made me double three times round the parade ground 'to warm your horrible great self up'.

We were warned not to gamble, light the stove before 1600 hours or remove an electric light bulb from its socket and ordered to have a bath at least once *each week*.

But the most sinister exhortations were legacies of the war that had ended three years earlier. 'Don't talk about the Service to strangers or in the hearing of strangers.' Enemy agents posing as village idiots, we were informed, might boast knowledge of damage at an airfield and trick the unwary into divulging the true details. 'GIVE THESE PEOPLE A WIDE BERTH.'

Since then I have regarded all the village idiots I have known – and there have a been a few – with the deepest suspicion.

The booklet also forbade us to thumb lifts. One of the reasons: 'The motorist may only be going a little way past where the airman is standing.'

Or he might have been going to Monte Carlo!

But I'm afraid my conscript's lament will never be published: the present is too urgent.

May 4.
Drive to Hartley, 70 miles from Salisbury, to hear Ian Smith talk. The bush is tanned by the sun, the sky hot and blue, the road straight and clear. The meeting is held on a rugby pitch in a little town populated by leathery men, farmers mostly, and women in garden-party dresses. They are right behind Smith, the Rhodesia Front and independence. The platform is festooned with bougainvillaea and copies of a new national anthem are available. The sky turns yellow, the evening is cold and iced with stars, smoke from barbecue fires drifts across the pitch. Smith is a better speaker than I had anticipated. A tallish man in a grey suit, one side of his face frozen − a legacy from the last war when, as a fighter pilot, he was wounded. He has a mild Rhodesian accent and does not pronounce the *g* in his *ings*. He tells these men and

127

women who made the bush flower that Rhodesia will declare
a unilateral declaration of independence − UDI − if negotiations with Britain finally collapse. After the meeting we
are expected to sing the new anthem; but a photographer
unplugs the loudspeaker system to connect floodlights and
we remain anthemless.

May 5.
Meeting contacts. John Monks, the staffer I am replacing,
takes me to a German photographer's house, thatched with
a swimming pool and acres of ground. In the evening Ian
Smith makes a dramatic announcement which to my new
ears sounds identical to all his other dramatic announcements.

May 6.
Meet Sir Roy Welensky. A bear of a man with tufted
eyebrows. He talks about world statesmen as I would talk
about the neighbours. He does not seem bitter about his
defeats in Rhodesia, but some anger must lurk beneath the
joviality. His devotion to his wife and family is one of his
most touching qualities. And he loves gardening.

In the evening I attend Ian Smith's last meeting before the
poll. It is packed with fanatical supporters, hairies as they
are known. He gets a tremendous ovation; but at a previous
meeting he was heckled into silence by students. He
announces that India has broken off diplomatic relations and
I rush to the office to file story on the Telex.

May 7.
Election Day. But there is little excitement in the streets,
broad enough for a bullock wagon to turn round in, or the
comfortable homes lounging in the tall-grassed outskirts of
town. The result is a forgone conclusion: victory for Smith
and his henchmen who are demanding speedy independence.
The women who wear Queen's Birthday clothes and teenage
hair-styles shop and drink coffee; their daughters ride or
play tennis, their menfolk grow tobacco, sell tobacco. I meet
a P.G. Wodehouse character who rides horses: what else he

128

does is not clear. He has a petulant brown face, nags away in a swallowed voice about his nags and is always ready for one-for-the-road, but it's a long, long road.

We start getting the election results at 10pm. There is a massive swing — swings are always massive — towards Smith and the Rhodesian Front. By midnight it looks as if he will grab all the European seats. Now there will be more negotiations with Britain but the hairies who voted for Smith will not tolerate much more procrastination.

May 8.
Twenty years ago I stood in Piccadilly Circus on VE Day with Peter Pritchard and Barrie Mullins. We were 15 and trying to drink the courage to kiss girls.

May 9.
Say farewell to John Monks at the airport. Diesel fumes, excess baggage, waiting with beers no one wants, neat-voiced announcements, aircraft with serpents' faces trundling along the tarmac, goodbye platitudes. On the verandah Africans sip beer and watch the planes go by; small black hands grab my trousers and I ruffle a baby's unrufflable hair; I smile at the mother but she doesn't smile back; she looks at me like a frightened cat whose kittens are being molested. A group of white Rhodesian girls in tight ski-pants and spun-sugar hair wave goodbye to the Argentine Rugby team which has been visiting Rhodesia.

John Monks strides out to the plane, a chunky figure, absolutely honest, absolutely dependable, weighed down with baggage. The aircraft gathers speed, soars into the yellow sky — FINIS. More final, more sad, than any smoke-billowing, handkerchiefed railway farewell.

Back in Salisbury I have a few drinks with an American agency man. He can fall asleep anywhere at any time. One minute he's conversing, 'Hi, father, is there no end to your grossness?' (that's how he talks) next minute he's lost in gentle, bubbling snores. We go into a multi-racial hotel for a drink and are told by the African behind the bar that we can't stay because we aren't wearing ties. 'Is there no end to this grossness, father?'

May 11.
Fly to Nairobi during a break in the Rhodesia story. It is one of my favourite cities, full of sunshine, flaking jacaranda and tongues of flamboyant, glorious girls and white hunters who are, in fact, brown and rather disappointing. Arrive in a VC-10 with Peter Younghusband, who seems to have grown since I last met him in West Africa when he was 6ft. 6ins., and book into a new African hotel redolent of new wood and loneliness.

May 12–14.
Nairobi's not the same, they say. But they say that in every city I've visited. 'You should have been here in the good old days.' Usually it is they who are not the same, and the days are still just as good. But Nairobi is in transition. Meet old friends: Jim Brown who came to my farewell party in London; Denis Neeld whom I last saw in Lagos; Peter Webb from *Newsweek*, last seen in Salisbury; Eric Downton from the *Telegraph*, last seen in London.

I sit at table around a thorn tree outside the New Stanley Hotel and watch the town pass by. Thick-limbed show-offs in aggressive bush shirts, tanned girls in silk blouses and tight trousers, wealthy Indian businessmen whose dignity has been imperilled by Peter Sellers, Africans bursting with equality, a beggar or two. Some white women still bawl kitchen Swahili at the stewards but there is a hollow ring to it. I meet one such lady from the bush, middle-ageing, trousered, bush-shirted, tanned, blonde and still attractive. 'Beer steward,' she bellows. And chunters away in Swahili although all the stewards speak English. 'Flew in this afternoon,' she announces. 'Bloody planes everywhere. Came in under them. Couldn't stay up there all day.' I gather she pilots a small plane. 'Drove from the airport like the clappers. Want to do all the night spots tonight. Long time since I was here. Must get pissed. More beer steward.'

130

And more Swahili. But her reign is being blown away by the wind of change.

Younghusband and Downton file a story about an abortive coup at Easter. I content myself with a story that all diplomats in Nairobi have been confined to a ten-mile radius of the city, and receive a cable dispatching me to Mauritius where a state of emergency has been declared. Speak to London on the phone in the evening and talk to photographer Harry Dempster, who says he will meet me at Nairobi Airport in the morning.

May 15.
Meet Harry, stocky, fair-haired and enthusiastic, at the airport and board a 707 for Mauritius via Tananarive. I sit beside a mustard salesman. We pass over the crinkled brown hills of Madagascar, watered by great rivers. Spend three hours at Tananarive then across the Indian Ocean to Mauritius via Réunion. A Tourist Board official meets us and we drive at a ridiculous speed through the town of Curepipe which is twenty-five minutes from everywhere on the island.

May 16.
Meet Frank Taylor, *Daily Telegraph* man based in Cape Town. We share common sense of humour, just as Harry Miller and I did in Cyprus. The Park Hotel has been transported from the Deep South of America: white colonnades, a terrace and big shuttered windows. It has about it an air of forgotten calm − like the island.

The island isn't much bigger than the Isle of Wight. It is covered with sugar cane as high as bungalows, prairies of it rustling in the winds from India and Australia. Roads cut swathes through the cane, women walk bowed down with great loads of it. It was here that the Dodo (as dead as) was said to have lived, poor thing that he was, unable to fly and clobbered as easily as a fat cumbersome duck. Cruel mountains as sharp as teeth spike the tall fields; the beaches are silver, fenced with palms, littered with coral and shells,

131

some of them patterned with tiny brown pyramids.

In the centre of the island it rains. On the shores the sun shines. We are met by a group of politicians and taken on a brain-washing tour of the island. The terrorists strike at night: they pile stones in the road to stop cars, beat the motorists or shoot them with spear guns and vanish into the sugar cane. Two men have so far been killed, one injured. Roughly speaking the warring factions are Indians and Creoles. The Creoles who want integration with Britain fear domination by the Hindus who want independence. The terrorists are said to be the Indians: I say this with reservations because we were told this by the Creoles. The King of the Creoles is Gaetan Duval, a thirty-three-year-old politician who manages to combine the duties of Minister of Housing, Town and Country Planning, Lands and Immigration. He is small and dark with a bandit's face; he rides around in a blue sports car with a French klaxon horn and some reckon he will be the next premier of Mauritius. He never seems to wear a suit, just blue jeans and an open shirt. It is unusual to find such a person being pro-British: he is the archetypal guerilla crouching behind a boulder, pulling the pin from a grenade with his teeth. But he preaches peace and is adored by the young people of Mauritius.

We are taken to a beach house for lunch and drinks. We swim in the blue water and chat to Duval and his henchmen bobbing around in the warm sea. I am unsure who is interviewing whom. 'You like it here?' he asks surfacing beside me. 'Don't be frightened of sharks. The only sharks here belong to the Labour Party.'

May 18.
This mildewed Isle of Wight set in the Indian Ocean pulsates with politics. And the hospitality of the politicians is inescapable. We have our ears bent by the heavy French accents of the Creoles and the intense lilts of the Indians — 'I am going to tell you, sir, that the trouble here is not racial. Not racial at all. I am going to tell you that it is political.' We escape in the afternoon and drive to a beach called Flic au

Flac. On the way back we see a rainbow arching across the island and melting into the sugar canes at our feet. We haven't time to search for the crock of gold.

In the evening we are taken to an annual club dinner. The club is formed for the furtherance of a multi-racial Mauritius. It reminds me of the annual bicycling dinners I once reported in Dartmouth and King's Lynn. Indians, Creoles, French and British make faltering, elaborate conversation. The guest speaker talks about tea with interruptions from a woman who looks like Hermione Gingold. The chairman tells a few jokes, so does a priest — the St. Peter and Heaven variety. A pretty Irish woman sings pretty Irish songs and there is a lot more ear bending before we leave in a blizzard of invitations. A lost evening.

May 19.

Attend the legislative assembly in an old white-painted, wooden building with blue ceilings. An avenue of palm trees leads up to it. Inside members debate vehemently beneath the fans in this tropical House of Commons. We lunch with some MPs and talk about sugar and politics; then escape once more to a beach.

In Curepipe and Fort Louis, the two towns, the old French colonial houses moulder behind bamboo hedges cut as sharply and squarely as privet in Muswell Hill. Trees whisper, the gardens flame with lilies quenched by cascades of morning glory. On the outskirts of the towns the tottering shacks are crammed with children. Women in pink and yellow saris float among the squalor like visiting angels, the dusk is scented with woodsmoke, the mountain peaks sharpen the skyline, waves rippling the seas of sugar spill on the roadsides.

May 20.

I walk into Curepipe for a coffee. The terraces of shops are discoloured by humidity, filled with Chinese, Hong Kong and Indian junk. A procession of old Indian women, bowed by loads of bamboo, and a patrol of sheepish British

133

Guardsmen pass by. A few French girls exaggeratedly chic in these surroundings zip around in fast cars. The air is musty, aromatic.

In the afternoon we attend a Press conference given by a Major Willoughby, officer commanding the Guards. He is neat and tough and wrinkles his nose when he smiles. One of his distant relatives fought a naval battle with the French here in 1810. His ship was sunk and he went into hospital with the French commander. He was later court-martialled, then knighted and has long been a revered black sheep in the Willoughby ancestry. The Guardsmen swim and ride but there is a dearth of that other essential military comfort, girls.

May 21.
I drive through sugar cane plantations to Le Mourne Plage. A little restaurant on the beach. A hill of black mildewed rock shadows the beach. The sand is deep, scattered with branches of coral like bones that tinkle when you kick them. Small fish jump over lava rocks, sea slugs writhe and pink starfish lie beaten among the crushed shells.

A mile out to sea waves try to reach the island through the coral reef and leap in walls of spray. Grey clouds hang wet and heavy and the surf beats muted funereal drums. Australian sailors from a survey ship drink beer in the hotel but even they are weighted with atmosphere.

May 22.
I walk round the grounds of the hotel. The bare-branched trees are furred with moss and lichen and the grey-green leaves breathe soulfully. Everything is damp to the touch, envelopes glue themselves together and the rain drifts in, touching palms and carob trees. We leave tomorrow.

May 24.
The Nairobi scene – prairie skies, iced beer, vacuous conversation, political rumours, teenagers hellbent on rowdy Saturday fun, Americans in safari hats trimmed with leopard

skin, beggars selling their deformities, curio shops selling masks and carvings and elephant hair bracelets, bougainvillaea in pastel orange and pink, flamboyant and jacaranda and pepper trees with soft tresses trailing in the breeze, the Norfolk swimming pool smelling of curry and tanning oil and chlorine and adorned with honey-coloured, bikini-trimmed flesh, Indian streets floating with saris.

May 27.
I am introduced to a woman who shoots game and sends specimens, hearts and arteries and suchlike to London for analysis. Her name is Miss Sykes; she is big, jovial and efficient. I interview her in a laboratory beside a pile of elephants' jawbones. Apparently poor old Jumbo resembles Man in many ways and it is therefore his fate to be shot. He suffers from hardening of the arteries and Miss Sykes sends lengths of artery to Britain to help scientists study the degenerative process. I ask her: 'Do you ever feel a twinge of compassion when you shoot an elephant?' She says: 'No, not really. I can't see that it's any different to killing rats or mice.' She shows me a jawbone − apparently an elephant's teeth slowly edge forwards down a sort of gulley until only one is left on either side of its mouth. When they have gone the elephant dies because he can no longer eat − unless he's already been clobbered by Miss Sykes.

She has in her time shot 25 elephants. She finally admits to regret one day when she shot a pregnant cow elephant. She shoots them through the brain, being careful to avoid the pituitary gland. She says: 'Had a nasty moment the other day. An elephant wounded with a bullet in the ear charged me from the bamboo forest. I let fly and brought it down six yards away.' She also takes sperm from freshly killed animals such as giraffe for artificial insemination. So animals caged in zoos will soon be giving birth without even the transient pleasure of procreation. Poor old Jumbo.

June 3.
Chou En-lai is visiting Dar-es-Salaam. I catch a VC-10 with

135

my old agency buddy, Jim Brown. We arrive to find Chinese frantically erecting red and yellow arches and draping the streets with paper flags. Dar is muggy compared with Nairobi. Have a quick swim at the Inn by the Sea – a pleasant barn of a place separated from the endless beach by palms and sand creepers. File a curtain-raiser from the New Africa Hotel. What on earth was the Old Africa Hotel like? We are given a tall old room with mosquito nets and fans. I drink in the moist air on the verandah, feeling Africa and the salt sea.

June 4.

I am awoken by an African with a cable. Back Nairobi soonest – Oginga Odinga has been stopped from representing Kenya at the Commonwealth Prime Ministers' Conference. But I still have time to see Chou En-lai arrive. I drive to the airport thick with crowds and flags and drum noises. An Ilyushin lands and out steps a frail figure with George Robey eyebrows quite unlike the virile figure we have been led to expect from photographs plastered around the town. Anthems, drums, studied formality, children with bouquets . . . Is there no other way to do it? Amid all the contrived festivity stands one symbol of permanency: an old, stiff-necked Rolls-Royce landau. And it is in this that Chou is driven into town. After much anguish I manage to catch a Fokker Friendship back to Nairobi where I have to file a feature off the cuff.

June 7.

Drinks in the Long Bar of the New Stanley where the white hunters meet. Meet a tall Scandinavian monkey catcher with pale blue eyes and a long sad face. He spikes bait with tranquillizers. He tells me: 'When the monkeys are drugged I sort them out, rejecting pregnant females, babies and old males.' Those he keeps are used for polio research, but the sad-faced hunter seems very fond of his quarry. He says he can get me a bush baby, but quarantine regulations in Britain are stringent so I'd better stick with the cat. I was drinking the other evening with a hunter when a bush baby popped out of his shirt and regarded me through big, lustrous eyes. It accompanies its master everywhere inside his shirt.

I also meet a genial, heavily-built Indian hunter and a pretty pert girl who confides that she is having a baby in September and she isn't married. 'Are you married or do you live in Nairobi?'

June 9.
Nairobi at dusk. The streets purr with homeward traffic and neon signs stutter in the fading light. The skyline is yellow and there are wet-dust scents in the air. Indians flit moth-like past their emporiums; arrogant Sikhs prowl the streets awaiting the predatory night. The air is soft and the martinis are cold and the sky is now the colour of a lion's mane. Hemingway's Africa; Robert Ruark's city.

June 12.
Dinner with Peter Webb, of *Newsweek*, and his wife. Gorgeous stew and dumplings. Peter Younghusband is there, and Lucy Hoare, the European who virtually runs Nairobi airport and is now leaving. The story goes that one of her forebears met Sam Goldwyn in America. After a pleasant evening Goldwyn said to this particular Hoare: 'And don't forget to give my regards to Lady W!'

Lucy, tall, witty and charming, tells stories of her experiences in Jerusalem. She was once met at the airport by an 18-year-old Arab who put his hand on her knee and said: 'I will make you very happy tonight.' Lucy replied that she did not want to be made happy. The Arab expressed surprise and said: 'I always made Mrs Warmington happy every evening – and sometimes in the afternoon as well.' She was also trapped in a hotel restaurant by the hotelier who in some inexplicable manner managed to grasp her tongue between his teeth. Lucy says you cannot scream if someone has your tongue between their teeth.

137

June 14.

With a monk at the controls and a famous pilot beside him, I fly north in a gnat-sized Cessna to see a Flying Nun. She is Sister Ryan, one of the Medical Missionaries of Mary. She runs a mission in the near-desert at Lorugumu and buzzes around spreading the good word in her own little aeroplane. The famous pilot is Max Conrad, who holds the round-the-world solo record. He has leathered skin and ice-blue eyes. He looks laconic but talks compulsively about aviation.

We flit over the green hills outside Nairobi, peering into villages of mushroom-shaped huts and sprawling farmhouses. Clouds touch us with feathery fingers as the countryside thins and toughens up. We land at Eldoret where there is a reception committee awaiting us (the aircraft was flown to Kenya from America by Conrad and was paid for by the United Missions Aviation Training and Transport – UMATT). Hundreds of black children and 50 or so European schoolgirls in red uniforms.

The monk, Brother Michael Stimec, takes locals for a couple of joy-rides and makes one appalling bouncing-ball landing. The children envelop the little aircraft, Conrad, Brother Mike and me. The girls in red demand autographs. I say gamely: 'You don't want mine – I'm no one.' They treat this as false modesty and rip pages from their scripture books for signing. So this is what it's like to be a Beatle.

We are then driven into the dusty town for Conrad to sign the Mayor's guest book. We make laboured conversation and then return to the plane accompanied by Catholic priests, mostly Irish, wearing crumpled grey suits and big dusty shoes. They are both rough and gentle and their humour is simple. We are joined by the Roman Catholic Bishop of Eldoret, Bishop Joseph Houlihan, from Bally-ferriter, Co. Kerry. His joke is that his name is not spelt Hooligan.

We fly over brown wastes cracked with ravines, furred with thorn trees, speared with razored mountains, until we reach a thirsty wilderness as desolate as anything I've seen.

138

We touch down on a desert airstrip watched by incurious camels, four nuns and another host of African children. The nuns are gay and skittish, bubbling with small jokes about religion and flirtation. Four Lilies of the Desert, but tough nuts just the same. Sister Ryan is an American with a handsome gentle face. She has 300 flying hours behind her. She tells me: 'I love flying but it can be alarming. The other day I landed while an electric storm was raging. I just managed to see the mission and put down before the full force of it hit me.'

Tukarna ladies are also there to meet us. They plait their hair with oil and leave their breasts bare. They also wear pellets of lead plugged into holes in their lower lips to prevent lockjaw. At first they allow photographs, but reluctantly as if even in this primeval place they suspect that ladies do not wear topless dresses. Then they disappear, swamped in giggles whenever a lens is aimed at them. Their menfolk spend much of their time fighting a neighbouring tribe because they cannot seek any of the lead-lipped girls' favours until they've proved their manhood. Kissing must present a problem.

The nuns take us to their mission, a small concrete block roofed with dazzling sheets of metal. They give us beer and roast lamb and flan and coffee and hover happily around plying us with more. Sister Mary Campion from Ipswich tells me: 'We have our problems here. The other day I was cornered in my room by a puff adder but luckily someone came in and frightened it away. We also have tidal waves that sweep down the dried-up river outside the mission. Once it washed me up a tree and I had to stay there for two days.' The Bishop, who is known as a 'character', makes Irish jokes and religious jokes and teases the nuns about going into retreat. I should have thought the mission was retreat enough.

Buffalo, monkeys and scorpions abound. And, farther north, Shifta raiders. They swarm over the Kenyan border caked in red mud, hair plaited with cow dung. They are

139

armed with Chinese weapons and like to mutilate their victims. It was at nearby Lodwar that Jomo Kenyatta was interned.

June 15.

Again a tiny aircraft which I have chartered this time. I fly with a reporter from the *East African Standard*, Derek Watkins, to Moshi, in Tanzania, to see Pat Hemingway, son of Ernest. We fly at giraffe height over the game park. Gazelle and zebra scatter, wildebeest chase their shadows, ostriches strut with arrogant unconcern. Kilimanjaro rears from the haze, a great sugar-cake of a mountain, its foothills clothed with bush that looks like broccoli from the air.

We have been warned by our pilot to expect tough immigration at Moshi. The single building is deserted and a lonely African says all he wants is the pilot's signature. We drive into town, drink a cold beer at the Livingstone Hotel, and head out to the College of Game Preservation where Hemingway teaches Africans to become game wardens. He is a small man dressed in a pink shirt, baggy trousers and greenish boots. There is a slight resemblance to his father in the roundish shape of the head. There the similarities end. He is now devoted to preserving wild life − although he still shoots elephants from necessity − whereas his father was devoted to extinguishing it. And here he is beneath the Snows of Kilimanjaro!

He tells me: 'It's pure coincidence that I came here − it's just that the college is here.' He used to be a white hunter but got bored with killing. He has a loud nervous laugh and speaks of his father with neither reverence nor contempt and he does not seem to be the victim of any of the complexes which supposedly afflict sons of famous men. He remembers Ernest as a good father who liked playing with his children and was always making jokes.

Pat is 36, his wife died a little while ago from cancer and his four-year-old daughter, Edwina, lives here with him beside Kilimanjaro. He tells me: 'I've never even climbed it.'

140

We tour the college, inhabited by stuffed animals and speared with horns. Pat tells me that during his last safari Ernest was struck with amoebic dysentry. He thinks this may have darkened some of his subsequent stories of death and hopeless passion. Despite the laugh and the dedication to his job I feel as he drives us to the airport through a coffee plantation a palpable sense of loneliness.

June 18.
Publication day of *The Sheltered Days* – and here I am 35,000 ft. high in a VC-10 flying over the Zambesi to Salisbury. And I haven't even got a copy! I drink champagne and eat ham sandwiches and hope queues are forming outside bookshops.

June 22.
Buy a car for £20. A small black and busted Morris Minor two-toned with rust; the sort of vehicle that one day parks itself in a farmyard and stays there until its skeleton turns to dust. Spend most of the morning taxing and insuring it. Salisbury is dull compared with Nairobi. I pay bills, answer letters, and wander around the skyscrapers squashed beneath the hot sky. The *Sunday Times* carries a review of my book, commenting that total recall is not always as effective as impressionism. Robert Pitman gives me a good write-up in the *Sunday Express*.

June 24.
This morning I want to gaze out of my window and see slate roofs wet with rain. Cats prowling, smoke knitted above steam trains. Or sunshine through transparent lime and burgeoning scents of haze and honey.

June 28.
I witness a cabaret at a night club that I confidently assert must be the worst in the world. Bill Bell of UPI says no, the cabaret at another club in Salisbury must be the worst. We stake bets, the winner to be adjudged – referees Mike

141

Keats and Peter Rackham, both of UPI. We visit Bill's club where they have what they call a sundowner show at 6.30pm. It is incongruous walking in from the sunlight into the stale, smoke-laced cavern of the club. But you soon forget the time: that's how it is, I suppose, with the girls in the caves in France whose reactions to submersion in the dark are being observed by scientists. First a coloured girl sings. I relax: my man is much worse than this. Then a girl dances under a flaming bar a few inches from the ground. The night is mine – and the £1. Bill looks ridiculously confident. At 11pm we adjourn to my club. My comedian imitates a dentist's drill, indulges in some smut and imitates a tenor suffering from hay fever. Bill orders a stiff drink and pays up.

The carnage continues in Saigon. Yesterday's papers carry pictures of a small child maimed and terrified by a bomb explosion. I cannot look at it.

July 5.
Marching orders to Johannesburg where the *Rand Daily Mail* editor and one of his reporters may be charged following an exposure of conditions in South African jails. The acacia trees in Salisbury are flushing autumnal brown, fragile reminders of the majestic reds and ochres of autumn in England. The nights are cold and instant darkness at 6.30pm after a day of sunshine is still a surprise. I shall miss the Saturday sale of cut flowers. The blooms sold by Africans form a herbaceous border of packed blossom along one side of Rhodes Square. Poppies with petals like crumpled butterfly wings, bunched chrysanthemums, stocks smelling of English gardens, African everlasting flowers.

July 6.
Fly to Johannesburg in a VC-10. What a rich, bustling place it is. I get the facts about the prison exposé – three articles describing in nauseating detail the lot of prisoners, particularly Africans – plus a telephone interview with the *Rand Daily Mail* editor. I also interview the reporter who compiled the

features from information supplied by a former prisoner.

July 7.
Return to Salisbury in a Viscount surrounded by children.
Give my best avuncular smile as a fourteen-month-old baby
girl beside me spits prune purée over my suit. On the other
side of an aisle a four-week-old baby sleeps and blows
slumberous bubbles. Every time I catch the young mother's
eye she beams with huge pride.

July 22.
Jim Brown and I drive 125 miles to the Mount Kenya Safari
Club. The road leads through the bush and red and green
hills planted with maize. Old women bent to the ground with
grass and firewood bundles meander along the roadside. We
stop for a beer at the Blue Posts Hotel in Thika, have a game
of darts and wander down to a waterfall fringed with trees
hanging with colobus monkeys.

As we approach Nyeri we start looking for Mount Kenya.
'Someone has removed it,' says Jim. I say: 'What a story.
And we've got it exclusively.' 'Not much use to you,' says
Jim, 'I'm an agency man — remember.' And a good one —
sharp and quick, still a little hollow-eyed from a bullet which
nearly killed him in the Congo.

On we drive, still no sign of Kenya's second highest
mountain. We turn on to a dust road where, to the right, the
skyline thickens beneath muddy grey clouds. This, it
transpires, is Mount Kenya.

The Safari Club is Hollywood Africa. A line of chalets
leads away from the clubhouse, each with its complement of
African servants. You say: 'Jambo,' and they say: 'Good
morning, sir.' The chalets have log fires spiralling sparks,
sunken baths, bowls of fruit, desks, easy chairs. We play a
round of clock golf. On one side of us the forest soars up to
the white teeth of the mountain; in the forest leopards blend
their spots with sun-dappled glades and lions with full bellies
blink lazily.

We swim in a star-shaped swimming pool heated to 78

degrees and regard each other through an observation window, an ugly sight. One of the owners, millionaire Ray Ryan, is a bird lover and the shaved lawns and chains of lakes are feathered with pink flamingos, maribou storks, cranes and peacocks who peer into the chalet windows. William Holden the film star has an interest in the club.

The sky darkens and scarves of cloud swathe the mountain peak. We meet the Swiss manager, floral-jacketed and solicitous. And the under-manager, lustrous-eyed and long-haired, who regards the most innocent question as a trick. 'Where is the sewage disposed of?' 'I'm afraid I can't answer that. But that's not for quotation. All I am permitted to say is, "No comment".' He would prosper in the Press section of any Ministry. We dine well and retire with promises of sauna baths and horse riding in the morning.

July 23.
Next morning we swim at 7.15am. The water is warm and the only cold portion of the anatomy is one's head. I eat a mango beside the pool and half an hour later get violent stomach pains. I retire to the toilet and then collapse on my bed where I discover that my body is covered with weals. I'm dripping with sweat; I try to feel my pulse but find none. Knife-edged pains stab my abdomen. The hotel management offers to call a doctor but I decline his services. While I suffer a boy in the chalet next door falls off his horse and breaks a leg. I recover by lunchtime and we drive back to Nairobi.

At the New Stanley I receive a cable telling me that the birth of my third child is imminent. I book myself on the London-bound VC 10 that night, Jim drives me to Embakarsi airport and once again I take to the sky in a blast of burned paraffin. A plaintive little Austrian woman sits next to me. She drinks whisky and tells me about her travels with her 'late husband'. They seem to have been inseparable. 'I always used to help him tether the yacht,' she says. She rejects the meal – 'My late husband always travelled top class' – and continues to drink Scotch. After a while the

144

buttons on her dress begin to pop. Before falling asleep she says: 'He was always late, the bastard.'

The button-popping reminds me irresistibly that among my acquaintances in Salisbury are a temperamental tassel-tosser and a bunny girl who asserts that she had the biggest bust in the Folies Bergère touring company; I see no reason to contest this. In Nairobi I knew Joan Rhodes, who was billed as the strongest girl in the world. On stage there was no reason to refute this either as, harnessed, she could pull a bevy of husky farmers across the stage of a night club.

July 24.
The gynaecological alarm was false. I drive my father, Patrick and Martin to Banstead Recreation Ground to watch Banstead play Surrey Club and Ground. In the High Street we see a man carrying a little girl step in front of a motorcycle. The motorcyclist falls off and rolls towards my car. He appears to be unhurt; the little girl has been taken into a shop. I give the motorcyclist my name and address because he may need an eye witness. He and the girl are taken to hospital. But what did I see? Did the motorcycle hit the girl or the man? Was the motorcyclist too near the kerb? Did the man fail to exercise sufficient caution? How frail is the divide between accuracy and inaccuracy in a courtroom and how comprehensively can an adroit lawyer manoeuvre an equivocal witness such as myself. And how abruptly can the serenity of a Saturday afternoon be shattered.

July 25.
Sunday. Genteel rain and sunshine. At 6.45pm a policeman rings and asks me to make a statement about the accident. While he's on his way the false alarm becomes genuine and I drive Elizabeth to hospital at Sutton. Return to Banstead nick and make a statement about the accident, apologising for my uncertainty. 'That's all right, sir,' says the policeman wearily. 'It's better than nothing.'

I return to the hospital and wait two hours in a waiting room. When I finally emerge a sister screams, then tells me

145

she thought I was a burglar — Matthew, 8lbs. 9ozs., had been born an hour and a half earlier and they had forgotten all about me. Mother and child doing well.

August 2.
Matthew doing extraordinarily well, book only moderately so, but the *South China Morning Post* seem to think it's okay. My father and I take the boys to Banstead cricket ground again. It is hedged grandly with chestnut trees and today the horizon is defended with castles of cumulus cloud. I enjoy Banstead. Tweedy women in little cars; coffee mornings; embroidered gardens; greengrocers that sell avocado pears and melons as well as brussels and spuds. The fathers who materialise on Saturdays in sports coats and flannels to take over the children and the dogs; the rows of semi-detacheds built in the '30s and grand detacheds with a second-hand Jag and a part-time gardener; the church which half-fills with bonnets and white gloves on Sunday morning while the roast is roasting, the flower show in the tent where the perfumes smell faintly like sweat.

Every day I wait for a call from the office informing me that some African Nationalist leader has been assassinated and will I get there as soon as possible.

August 11.
The call comes. Johannesburg. At London Airport I meet Fleet Street colleagues and competitors covering a story about a kidnapped baby. Fly by Caravelle to Brussels, fed on smoked salmon and wined on champagne by a big blonde Sabena hostess in a pale blue uniform. Board a 707 and whoosh into the darkening sky on the way to Athens. A long sticky wait glowering at everyone and inspecting the expensive and useless knick-knacks on display. Drop a cowbell which makes a terrible clatter. Everyone stares and I continue to glower as William does in Richmal Crompton's books. On towards Léopoldville, sleeping fitfully. Finally fall into a deep sleep only to be awoken by bow-tied steward serving orange juice and breakfast — two fried eggs stuck

146

together like mating jellyfish. We descend over the broad, brown Congo littered with islands like stepping stones. The vegetation is bright green and I imagine I can see crocodiles.

Léopoldville airport, scene of so much anguish over the past five years, is dawn-hushed and shabby. I wait in the transit lounge sipping a sickly orange drink and reading *The Luck of Ginger Coffey* which overwhelms me with sadness; thank God for a fairly happy ending. A good book, though, reaching the core of male vanity, his often misguided optimism, his ability to shelve decision. For once the sex is a natural ingredient of the story: not *inserted* for its own sake. Zoom on to Johannesburg making stilted conversation with a Belgian sugar grower from the Congo. Eighteen and a half hours ago I was relaxing in high summer; now I am in winter and the trees are bare.

I walk around shabby back streets where Africans play cards on the corners and their women lean indolently against walls. Have a drink in a flea-bitten bar, stark and ugly, built for drinking and nothing else, before retiring to bed and sleeping for nine hours.

August 19.
Never judge a country or a city (or a person?) at first glance. Suddenly I am at one with Johannesburg. It is embalmed in sunshine as fragile as a September in England; the leafless trees are tipped with green fire; bushes printed with white and pink blossom, and the streets are peppered with the gritty determination that made it all possible.

August 20.
An early morning flight to Kimberley. Karen Muir, the 12-year-old South African girl who smashed the world women's back-stroke 120 yards record, has returned home. It's ä dusty little town. Incredible to think that it harbours such crystalline wealth beneath its crust. Bands play as Karen, staring at her feet, arrives in a large car outside her school. Since she arrived home she has done little but cry. Adults emphasise that she should be left alone to make a natural

recovery from the fame thrust upon her at twelve; then they set about doing the reverse.

Torrents of words from a platform outside the school; they are genuine in their pleasure at Karen's success but egoism cannot be subdued; they make their jokes, push their own causes. Karen twists around and stares with embarrassment at her school friends. In the background Africans loll in the sun: it's an occasion, no matter what, and should be enjoyed in sun-warmed indolence.

Then Karen is forced to speak. She does not know what to say, the headmaster prompts her; everyone giggles; poor little girl. I meet the headmaster's wife, powder-blue suit, little white hat and white gloves. She sits beside me and says in broadest Afrikaans: 'I'm sorry I don't speak good English.' But she is pert and pretty and who does speak English as she should be spoke?

Nearly everyone in Kimberley speaks Afrikaans. The town is as hard as diamonds, as sweaty as the toil that produces them. Big hats, chunky faces, pudding-basin haircuts. On the way back to Johannesburg in a four-seater Piper Comanche we fly over the diamond mines scooped from the blue-green soil and dip low over the extinct mine in the centre of town known as the Big Hole. Other mines, however, are bigger – gaping pits from which stones, now encrusting crowns, glittering on slim fingers or sulking in vaults have been dug over the decades. If all the reserves were released on the world market diamonds would be practically valueless. But who wants that? Why spoil the sparkling legend? Diamonds are for ever.

Two hours later we drop down over the gold mines of Jo'burg. From the air they look like sand castles patted flat with spades. In the evening I go to the cinema with Frank Taylor to see *How to Murder your Wife*. In South Africa a visit to the cinema is still the occasion it once was in Britain, one of the benefits of no television. It evokes memories of old, two-feature, celluloid-smelling picture houses; sonorous-voiced travelogues in which blossom swayed in perpetual motion; chocolate ice-creams dripping on your knees to the

148

strains of a Hammond organ; portrait galleries of the stars smiling winsomely; Humphrey Bogart and Errol Flynn and Joan Fontaine, with whom I was in love; usherettes in gold blouses and bell-bottom blue slacks whose torches we teenagers stole.

Like Harry Miller, Frank Taylor is the complete *Telegraph* reporter. Tall, fair-haired and deceptively dreamy-eyed — he writes poetry in his spare time — he can knock out a couple of columns of accurate, penetrating copy in the time it takes me to produce a ten-paragraph *Express* story. Readers of the *Telegraph*'s elegant pages would, I feel, be astonished by the rumbustious presence of some of its writers. How does the reader on the 8.45 Banstead–London Bridge train envisage Henry Miller who has written such an authoritative report on the front page? Certainly not playing bar football, a grenade's throw from Murder Mile in Cyprus.

September 15.
I have moved into the house rented by Mike Keats of UPI, who has taken over from Bill Bell, and his wife Sybil. Mike is a tough, prodigiously industrious Australian; Sybil is a South African with lovely eyes. She is also a superb cook and Mike and I become so glossy that we are known as Tubs I and II. They live in a small colonial house set in a big dusty tree-filled garden in a well-heeled suburb of Salisbury.

September 17.
The hairies are aptly named. I meet one in the back bar of Meikles. His arms, legs and the V of his neck are thick with hair; his head is bald. He talks about Rhodesia's future aggressively but defensively. 'Look what happened in the Congo, man. Would you hand your country over to the munts?' When he learns I am from the *Express* which is pro-Smith his truculence abates. But, of course, he makes the familiar mistake of assuming that a reporter shares the political views of his newspaper. I know many good Tories on the *Mirror* and many a committed Socialist on the *Express*. Hypocrisy? I don't think so; all the reporters I

149

know try to record events objectively; I certainly do but then my views have always been blunted by my tendency to view a battlefield from both camps. My hirsute companion scratches his chest and then his head as though trying to transfer some of the hair.

The story staggers on. Will Smith declare UDI or won't he? I assume he will because his views and the views of the British Government are intractable, but I wish he would get on with it — after a while small-town trivia and colonial rule without the romance and humour of, say, India squeeze the spirit out of you. At least my hairy friend didn't prevaricate.

September 19.
Sitting in the Keats' garden as the evening sky turns saffron and the insects start to sing in the flat-topped trees. Saffron to orange and the dusk lacquers the tall gum trees beyond into black trellis. Orange to ochre to purple; the evenings are sudden and tranquil. Televisions stutter into life — *The Planemakers*, *Danger Man*, the amateurish newscasts and interviews, the appalling advertisements. Night, heavy-breathing and rain-smelling. The weekend is over. Smith has made yet another my-patience-is-exhausted speech; Rhodesians have once again applied themselves to leisure with studied application — boating and barbecues and boozing. The sergeants' mess at the end of the Raj. And it all palls beside the potential enormity of the Indo-Pakistan War.

September 25.
Bruised clouds gather, lightning laces them. Blobs of rain spatter the dusty garden, filling the air with whitewash scents. Sybil and I go next door to listen to records in a house occupied by a girl named Anita who designs dresses. The rooms are dark and cool, floors parquet, walls hung with tapestries reminiscent of the ante-room of a stately home on visiting day. She plays part of *Under Milk Wood* on her super stereophonic record-player. Dylan Thomas's donnish voice recorded accidentally on a tape recorder in America floats in the gloom. But the performance does not

150

compare with the Richard Burton version which I first heard on an ancient wireless in digs in King's Lynn when I worked on the *Eastern Daily Press*. The Burton rendering soared and trembled with valley voices; the voices accompanying Thomas are flat and unresponsive.

We return to *our* house under dripping trees where I find a letter telling me that *The Sheltered Days* has been serialised on *Woman's Hour* on BBC radio. Each episode was introduced with a tune from the war concluding with Vera Lynn singing 'There'll always be an England'. Letters of appreciation of the series have since been read.

After Dylan Thomas the three of us visit friends of the Keats to play roulette. We eat curry and inevitably discuss racialism, garden boys, would you let your daughter marry an African, etcetera.

October 7.
An African spring. For three days we have shivered under a belly of grey cloud. Today the sun is shining and the streets are tunnels of jacaranda blossom which covers lawns with mauve snow. Every journalist manages to get jacaranda into his stories. Cyril Aynsley of the *Express* once claimed that he got it into every story he wrote about Rhodesia. I have not made up my mind about jacaranda; every tree is a leafless cloud of mauve, no variation in colour; it reminds me of boiled sweets.

The trees in the Keats' garden are in leaf now and bright birds with long tails hover among them. Elsewhere cheap-scented syringa and bottle-brush and hibiscus painted by Alice in Wonderland's gardeners are in flower. But none of it compares with the fragile graces of an English spring day.

The story has temporarily switched to London while Ian Smith and his boys confer in London. UDI . . . To be or not to be. Everyone asks me but I don't have the political insight of, say, David Adamson of the *Telegraph*. (He has had a book published too and we hold literary discussions after ferocious games of badminton.) My replies disappoint but I really don't know and I doubt whether Smith does either.

151

October 8.
Off to the trots, racing in which horses pull tiny chariots mounted by cumbersome jockeys in a floodlit stadium. The Tote is a trestle-table, the payout desk, which I rarely visit, is a hut. There are two bookies who regard each other with suspicion and another trestle-table from which warm beer is sold. The chariots wobble behind prettily-trotting horses: if they canter or gallop the jockeys have to brake. The climax of each race is a nightmare in which speed is gummed with sleep. Occasionally temptation overcomes a horse and it breaks into a gallop that no jockey can restrain. Result: disqualification. Just like UDI.

October 9.
Smith has walked out of the London talks. He says that UDI seems to be the only solution 'at the moment'. There is always a qualification. No doubt, though, that the crisis is reaching its climax. There is talk of war, economic starvation, United Nations intervention. Symbolically a thunderstorm cracks overhead at lunchtime. I shelter from the shotgun rain in the doorway of the cathedral and smell jacaranda and incense mingling.

October 15.
My first apartheid experience — in an African township! I take a taxi to Highfield with Michael Lake of the *Sun* and visit a beer hall with the driver, an African named David, who lives here. The Africans drink a beer brewed for them by the municipal authority; it is thick and pink, clogged with husks and vegetable matter. It costs 3d. a pint but customers usually buy a shilling's worth and drink it from large plastic containers. It tastes like a vinegar milkshake. We are regarded with curiosity and faint hostility. *Beer hall* evokes a tavern swimming in slops, boisterous and seedy; this is clean and spacious.

Most Africans drink in the garden but there is a chromium bar upstairs. We climb the stairs with David and meet the

152

manager who informs us apologetically that we will have to leave: the law states that Europeans must not drink in African beer halls!

We wander round a market where convicts work in the background. Children giggle and pose, hugging themselves with glee, for photographs. The stallholders say they only sell vegetables to help their husbands pay the rent. They all want land, they say, on which to grow their own vegetables. The township is a huge sprawl of houses that look like brick-built pre-fabs. The cheapest cost £1.10s. a month but some Africans earn only £10 a month. There is much evidence of poverty but no squalor. Some of the houses costing £12 a month are quite smart, like small bungalows built for retired couples behind Brighton. A TV aerial sprouts from one. I drive from Highfield to Highlands, one of Salisbury's pukka European residential areas where every house is accompanied by a swimming pool.

October 19.
News broke yesterday evening that Garfield Todd, former Prime Minister of Southern Rhodesia, has been placed under restriction. A convoy of us leaves Salisbury at 2am on a 250−mile drive to Shabani where Todd has a ranch. Jim Biddulph drives while I doze, waking occasionally to glance at the moonlit, skeletal bush. We stop for dawn tea at Shabani, a bleak, wild-west town buttressed by the pit-head hills of asbestos mines. Todd is not shy of publicity and, anticipating Press coverage, has chalked white arrows on the road pointing to the ranch. We bump along a dust track winding through dust-dry bush and suddenly there is the ranch-house, a floral oasis on the top of a ridge overlooking a brown river where hippos play.

Todd is a handsome, greying-haired man, dignified and articulate. We are overwhelmed with hospitality and sip our tea smugly as carload after carload of late arrivals drive up. Todd is confined to the area of his farm which happily for him is immense. He believes he has been restricted because he was on his way to Britain to appear on TV to air his

153

liberal views which are anathema to the Rhodesian Government. My contacts, however, tell me there were other reasons but they do not elaborate.

October 23.
The tempo of the story is at last hotting up. Harold Wilson arrives in Salisbury tonight in a last bid to find a basis for negotiation on independence. We understand that UDI would already have been declared if it hadn't been for his visit. By lunchtime there are some 2,000 Africans at the airport. Some have paid a shilling for a grandstand view from the balcony; others sweat it out on the grass. The dudes shelter beneath bright golfing umbrellas: the unassuming shade themselves with fronds of pale leaves. Wilson's white Comet roars in on time, excitement rises, the Africans chant and wave their banners. The sun sets sombrely, the sky is chipped with stars.

Wilson gives a Press conference, handling questions adroitly. A cute, canny little man who employs North Country humour to parry awkward thrusts and give himself time to think. I whistle our political correspondent, Wilfred Sendall, who arrived an hour earlier, back into Salisbury to file on the Telex.

October 23–30.
A whirlwind of Press conferences, lobby briefings, demonstrations, communication breakdowns, panic and pandemonium. There are more than 200 Pressmen in town. The negotiations become more complex every day and not even the pundits pretend to understand them. One day restricted African nationalist leaders arrive at Government House. Some 2,000 Africans massed outside to chant and dance. Then police dogs move in and terror replaces gaiety.

November 5.
The Governor declares a state of emergency and a new exciting element enters the story. I Telex an early piece in the belief that censorship may be imposed.

154

The Guy Fawkes dusk thickens, rockets explode like melting tinsel. I go to David Adamson's place to help let the fireworks off. In England now — two hours behind Rhodesia — mufflered, wellington-booted figures are haunting their gardens waiting for their fathers to put match to gunpowder.

November 6.
The state of emergency is something of an anti-climax. The bars are full of hard drinkers although theoretically the bars could be closed under the emergency regulations; Saturday-shopping housewives gather to discuss the Sunday joint although theoretically a gathering of more than three is illegal.

November 10.
The days have melted into a timeless flurry of sojourns outside the cabinet office, Smith speeches on TV, cold beers and swift Scotches, Jo'burg and London phone calls, play cables, queries and rumours. Every day we stand outside the cabinet office. Smith makes a few small jokes.'What are you doing down there?' pointing at a squatting photographer attempting a Hitchcock shot. Or 'Where are you going to get your film from now?' after new import controls have been announced. He seems to be harassed by his own party extremists, suspecting that UDI is national suicide.

November 11.
Smith does it. After the months of waiting it's rather an anti-climax. Then the communications nightmare begins. I file a quick take on Telex but developments overtake you as you write. The building chatters with Telex and my desk disappears under sheafs of handouts. I file through Jo'burg but ultimately it doesn't matter because everything gets out on Telex.

In Salisbury belt-tightening restrictions including possible rationing are announced. The spirit of defiance is still abroad in the tough little bars but it is a mite subdued now. In

London Wilson announces savage sanctions. Journalistically there is a feeling of relief that it has happened. The story will now endure for months, years.

November 12.
I drive to the airport to pick up Terry Fincher who has flown out from London. It's always reassuring to see his sturdy figure. He's just completed a parachute course to enable him to drop on stories with the paras.

The day passes in a welter of follow-ups, new leads. In the evening I get the first newspaper interview with Smith; Mike Keats gets the first agency exclusive. Smith answers my questions quietly, thoughtfully and with more dignity than is being evinced in Whitehall at the moment. His face is strained and he is choked with influenza. I ask him about his feelings when he severed his country from Britain. He says: 'It was the most emotional moment of my life.'

November 13.
Mike Keats wakes me at 6.30am after four hours sleep and asks: 'Do you want to fly to the Victoria Falls?' One hour later Mike and I and South African photographer Ernie Christie are buzzing over the bush in a tiny aircraft on our way to the Falls. At one stage we have to skirt a storm — over, under, around, the pilot tries everything to circumvent it and finally succeeds. In the distance I spot a plume of smoke rising from the bush: it is the spray from the Falls.

We put down at the small airstrip and drive across a bridge spanning a gorge — the vital link between Zambia and Rhodesia — and enter Zambia. Black Zambian troops commanded by white officers are digging in. They are very friendly and pose for pictures. Monkeys patrol the roadside in single file as if they are imitating the troops. We adjourn to a restaurant beside the mud-brown Zambesi. As we drink glasses of milk, hippos surface and the Falls thunder like distant gunfire. We return to the bridge and find Zambian and Rhodesian officers peering at each other through binoculars. This must be the most spectacular border post and the most incongruous confrontation of troops in the world. The officers, some of whom served with each other before the breakup of the Federation, greet each other across the bridge.

Back on the Rhodesian side police take a roll of film from Ernie Christie because they think he may have been photographing their troop positions.

I take a last look at the Falls. The mile-wide wall of water across the Zambezi which Livingstone named after his Queen in 1855 was aptly named by the Africans living there — the smoke that thunders. Like the stars the Falls dwarf mankind's endeavours and defy description. And diaries. It is time to finish.

POSTSCRIPT

After Africa I was posted to Moscow for what proved to be one of the most entertaining and productive years of my life. I returned to Britain smitten by what Soviet doctors diagnosed as rheumatic fever but which was subsequently denounced in Harley Street as gout. Having begun in Russia a novel, *Angels in the Snow*, and sensing that anti-climax could only follow such a cretinous departure from foreign coverage, I adjourned to the Irish village of Ballycotton, near Cork, where in rooms above Mrs Roberts' grocery shop, fuelled on draught Guiness, I set about becoming a novelist.

Thirty books later — a shelf that includes three precocious autobiographies and a series of historical thrillers about a Bow Street Runner named Blackstone written under the pseudonym Richard Falkirk — I have achieved a life of fulfilment aided and abetted by my second wife, Diane, whose understanding of a writer's crises has recently been broadened by her emergence as a journalist writing for an English-language magazine in Spain, *Lookout*. Our life has leisured comparisons with the frenetic days chronicled in the diaries: we have lived in many lands, we still travel extensively and we are both slaves of deadlines. Perhaps I should start recording our experiences for publication in the year 2007. . . .